Intermediate
Excel 365

EXCEL 365 ESSENTIALS - BOOK 2

M.L. HUMPHREY

CONTENTS

CONTENTS (CONT.)

Introduction

This book is the second in the Excel 365 Essentials series. If you're new to Excel then you're going to want to start with *Excel 365 for Beginners* because that book covers 95% of what you need to know to use Microsoft Excel on a daily basis, including the basics of entering information, formatting it, and using sorting, filtering, and basic formulas to analyze that information.

What this book does is covers topics that are more advanced than that, but still core skills that will help you use Excel on a daily basis, such as charts, pivot tables (which Excel likes to write as pivottables, but which drives me batty to write that way so I'm going to refuse to), and conditional formatting.

I'm also going to touch on the topic of pivot charts, which are charts you create from a pivot table, something I didn't do in *Intermediate Excel* or *Excel 2019 Intermediate*, the precursors to this book.

We'll also cover a few other useful but not essential topics like inserting symbols and equations, grouping data, subtotaling data, removing duplicate values, converting text to columns, fixing numbers that are stored as text, using the quick access toolbar, Excel Options, and zooming.

Most of what this book will focus on are core functions of Excel that have and will remain fairly stable over time. Excel 365 is a constantly-evolving product, but I don't expect it will evolve at any point in the near-term to make the information in this book outdated. Appearances may change a bit, but the core functionality should not. (And if it does, I'll unpublish this book because I don't want to be selling you information you can't use.)

This book does not cover formulas and functions at all, because the third book in the series, *102 Useful Excel 365 Functions*, is completely devoted to formulas and functions.

Okay. With that all said, let's get started. First things first, let's do a quick recap of the terminology that was introduced in *Excel 365 for Beginners* and then we can dive in with our first big topic, conditional formatting.

Basic Terminology Recap

Most of these terms were already defined in detail in *Excel 365 for Beginners*, so this is just to refresh your recollection.

Workbook

A workbook is what Excel likes to call an Excel file.

Worksheet

Excel defines a worksheet as the primary document you use in Excel to store and work with your data. A worksheet is organized into Columns and Rows that form Cells. A workbook can contain multiple worksheets.

Columns

Excel uses columns and rows to display information. Columns run across the top of the worksheet and, unless you've done something funky with your settings, are identified using letters of the alphabet.

The first column in a worksheet will always be Column A. And the number of columns in your worksheet will remain the same, regardless of how many columns you delete, add, or move around. Think of columns as location information that is actually separate from the data in the worksheet.

Rows

Rows run down the side of each worksheet and are numbered starting at 1 and up to a very high number. Row numbers are also locational information. The first row will always be numbered 1, the second row will always be numbered 2, and so on and so forth. There will also always be a fixed number of rows in each worksheet regardless of how many rows of data you delete, add, or move around.

Cells

Cells are where the row and column data comes together. Cells are identified using the letter for the column and the number for the row that intersect to form that cell. For example, Cell A1 is the cell that is in the first column and first row of the worksheet.

Click

If I tell you to click on something, that means to use your mouse (or trackpad) to move the cursor on the screen over to a specific location and left-click or right-click on the option. If you left-click, this selects the item. If you right-click, this generally displays a dropdown list of options to choose from. If I don't tell you which to do, left- or right-click, then left-click.

Left-click/Right-click

If you look at your mouse you generally have two flat buttons to press. One is on the left side, one is on the right. If I say left-click that means to press down on the button on the left. If I say right-click that means press down on the button on the right.

Select

If I tell you to "select" cells, that means to highlight them. You can either left-click and drag to select a range of cells or hold down the Ctrl key as you click on individual cells. To select an entire column, click on the letter for the column. To select an entire row, click on the number for the row.

Data

Data is the information you enter into your worksheet.

Data Table

I may also sometimes refer to a data table or table of data. This is just a combination of cells that contain data in them.

Arrow

If I tell you to arrow to somewhere or to arrow right, left, up, or down, this just means use the arrow keys to navigate to a new cell.

Cursor Functions

The cursor is what moves around when you move your mouse or use the trackpad. In Excel the cursor changes its appearance depending on what functions you can perform.

Tab

I am going to talk a lot about Tabs, which are the options you have to choose from at the top of the workspace. The default tab names are File, Home, Insert, Page Layout, Formulas, Data, Review, View, and Help. But there are certain times when additional tabs will appear, for example, when you create a pivot table or a chart.

(This should not be confused with the Tab key which can be used to move across cells.)

Dropdown Menus

A dropdown menu is a listing of available choices that you can see when you right-click in certain places such as the main workspace or on a worksheet name. You will also see them when you click on an arrow next to or below an option in the top menu.

Dialogue Boxes

Dialogue boxes are pop-up boxes that contain additional choices.

Scroll Bars

When you have more information than will show in a screen, dialogue box, or dropdown menu, you will see scroll bars on the right side or bottom that allow you to navigate to see the rest of the information.

Formula Bar

The formula bar is the long white bar at the top of the main workspace directly below the top menu options that lets you see the actual contents of a cell, not just the displayed value.

Cell Notation

Cells are referred to by their column and row position. So Cell A1 is the cell that's the intersection of the first column and first row in the worksheet.

When written in Excel you just use A1, you do not need to include the word cell. A colon (:) can be used to reference a range of cells. A comma (,) can be used to separate cell references.

When in doubt about how to define a cell range, click into a cell, type =, and then go and select the cells you want to reference. Excel will describe your selection in the formula bar using cell notation.

Paste Special Values

Paste Special Values is a way of pasting copied values that keeps the calculation results or the cell values but removes any formulas or formatting.

Task Pane

On occasion Excel will open a task pane, which is different from a dialogue box because it is part of the workspace. These will normally appear on the right-hand side in Excel for tasks such as working with pivot tables or charts or using the built-in Help function. (They often appear on the left-hand side in Word.)

They can be closed by clicking on the X in the top right corner.

Conditional Formatting

What is conditional formatting and why might you want to use it?

Conditional formatting is a way to take a data set and apply special formatting to certain results. It makes it much easier to see patterns as well as sort and filter your data.

I often will use conditional formatting in conjunction with a two-variable analysis grid. For example, I might build a grid with number of hours worked across the top and hourly pay rate down the side to see which combinations of hours and pay let me reach my income goal.

Let's say you need to make $500 a week. (I know, I wish that were how the world still worked, but just stay with me here.) Here's what I would put together for something like that:

		C	D	E	F	G	H
		Hours Per Week					
		15	20	25	30	35	40
	$ 15.00	$ 225.00	$ 300.00	$ 375.00	$ 450.00	$ 525.00	$ 600.00
Pay Rate	$ 20.00	$ 300.00	$ 400.00	$ 500.00	$ 600.00	$ 700.00	$ 800.00
	$ 25.00	$ 375.00	$ 500.00	$ 625.00	$ 750.00	$ 875.00	$1,000.00
	$ 30.00	$ 450.00	$ 600.00	$ 750.00	$ 900.00	$1,050.00	$1,200.00

I've applied conditional formatting to Cells C3 through H6 so that I can quickly see which combinations of hours per week and pay get me to that goal. 35 or 40 hours per week gets me there for all of the pay rates in the table. But if I can only work 20 hours a week, then I need to be paid $25 an hour or more.

Another place I use this is in my budgeting spreadsheet. There I have my bank account balance set with conditional formatting so that if I ever drop below the minimum balance for free checking, I can immediately see that and fix it before I end up paying an unexpected monthly account fee.

And I use this for the table where I list my revenue, ad spend, and profit from writing each month. I have it set so that each of those fields is shaded from light to dark so that I can easily see the months when I earned the most or least, the months when I spent the most or least on ads, and the months when I was most or least profitable.

That lets me spot trends across the months without looking at eight years' worth of numbers. I don't need to get hung up on the difference between $453.22 and $525.21 when I'm trying to look at trends.

I have another place where I don't even show the numbers at all. I have it set up to display colored bars instead. That lets me easily see how seasonal my results are. (Some products, like winter coats, sell better at certain times of year than others, right? The same thing can happen with different types of books.)

It can be useful to understand those patterns in your own business so that you plan accordingly. I always feel really good in January because that's a strong sales month for my books, but then I feel despair in July, which is not. Having conditional formatting to highlight the annual patterns in my sales reminds me that "this too shall pass", both the good months and the bad ones.

For a more traditional business, you could use conditional formatting to flag customer payments that are more than thirty days overdue. Or to highlight your largest sales transactions. Or flag any expense over $X which should have required pre-approval.

The possibilities are endless.

Another really great thing about conditional formatting is that you can combine it with filtering. So you could flag any customer payments that are overdue and then filter thousands of rows of customer data to only show those entries.

Now that you understand what conditional formatting is and how it works, let's walk through the various options you have in Excel.

First things first, to apply conditional formatting, select the cell range you want to use, and then go to the Styles section of the Home tab and click on the arrow for the Conditional Formatting option to show your available choices:

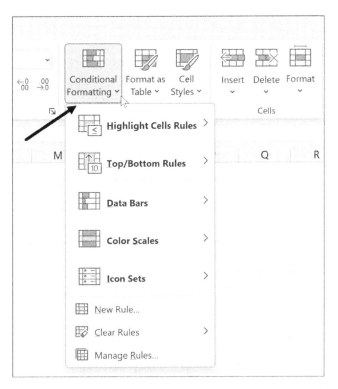

Your other option is to use the Quick Analysis button. To use this, highlight your cell range. You should then see a little icon appear in the bottom right corner of the selected range. Click on that and you'll see the Quick Analysis options.

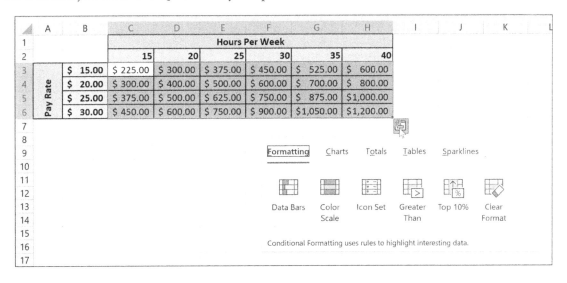

The Formatting tab is the one to use for conditional formatting. Move your mouse over those options and it will show you a preview on your data of what that will look like. The available options are going to depend on the nature of your selected data.

For text entries your options will be Text, Duplicate, Unique, Equal To, and Clear. For entries that contain text and numbers or numbers only, your options will be Data Bars, Colors, Icon Sets, Greater, Top 10%, and Clear.

Quick Analysis comes with its own preset styles that it's going to apply. If you like those styles, then it's a good option. I, at least for the greater than option and the way I use it, always have to change it from the default.

So I'm going to focus from here on out on how to apply conditional formatting using the top menu option, but do know that the quick analysis option exists and may be a quicker choice if you're willing to work with the default settings.

If you ever accidentally end up opening that quick analysis option when you didn't want to (which I have done off and on for years now), use the Esc key to close it. Your cells will remain selected but you won't have to choose one of those options.

Okay. Let's now walk through the conditional formatting dropdown menu from top to bottom.

Highlight Cells Rules

The highlight cells rules are what I used for the example above. What this section does is allows you to apply formatting to cells that meet certain criteria.

Here you can see the set of choices available via the dropdown menu:

You can choose from Greater Than, Less Than, Between, Equal To, Text That Contains, A Date Occurring, and Duplicate Values. There's also a More Rules option at the bottom that will open the New Formatting Rule dialogue box.

The option I used above was Greater Than (with an edit to make it Greater Than or Equal To), so let's click on that. It brings up the Greater Than dialogue box and immediately colors your selected range of cells based on the default criteria it comes up with and the default format:

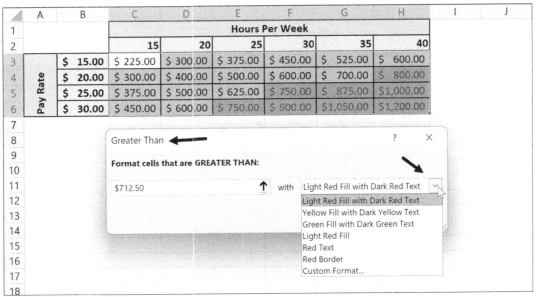

You can see here it went with greater than $712.50 and the default format is always going to be (or at least has been for decades) Light Red Fill with Dark Red Text.

Not what we want. Click into the box with the value and type in a new value. And then from the dropdown for the format you can either select one of the other options, I used Green Fill with Dark Green text above, or you can go to Custom Format and apply any formatting you want.

For a quick and dirty analysis I would likely type 499.99 into that box, choose the green formatting option, and be done. That's close enough to $500 or more and the fastest way to get my result.

But if it really matters that you have conditional formatting for $500 or more, then the default choices in that dropdown menu under Highlight Cells Rules aren't going to work.

You'll need to use the More Rules option at the bottom of the dropdown menu to have more choices. That, as I mentioned above, opens the New Formatting Rule dialogue box. By opening it through the Highlight Cells Rules dropdown it opens directly onto the "Format Only Cells That Contain" view:

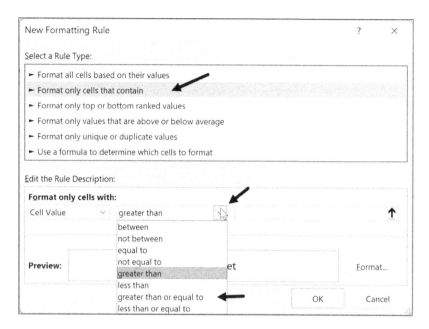

From there you can use the dropdown menu in that dialogue box to choose the "greater than or equal to" option and enter your specific value

But this way of applying a rule doesn't come with preset formatting to choose from like the options available through the Highlight Cells Rules dropdown.

To apply formatting, click on Format to open the Format Cells dialogue box.

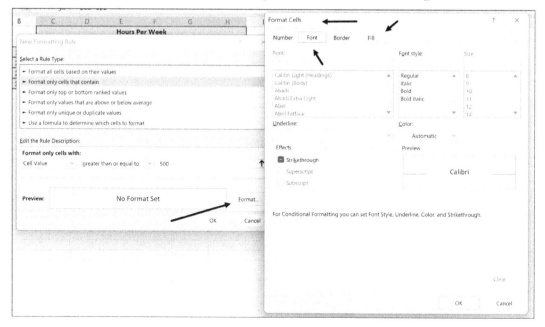

It opens onto the Font tab. That's where you can set the font color and any bolding or underline. But if you want to add a fill like the examples above use, then you'll also need to go to the Fill tab and choose a fill color from there. You cannot edit font or font size but most everything else is available to you.

When you're done click OK.

(Another option if you like Excel's default formats that we'll discuss later is to use one of the default options above, like Greater Than, apply one of the Excel formats, like the green text/green fill one, and then choose to Manage Rules and change the Greater Than option to the Greater Than or Equal To option at that point. That's how I did it. But we're not there yet.)

So. To summarize. Highlight Cells Rules for numbers come with a handful of default choices that you can access through that secondary dropdown menu. If you go that route you also have a handful of pre-defined formats you can apply.

But if you want more options, you need to use the More Rules choice and then you'll have to customize the formatting yourself.

Now let's talk about those bottom three options, Text That Contains, A Date Occurring, and Duplicate Values. I want to start with Duplicate Values because that can still be a numbers one.

Here I've selected Duplicate Values for this range of cells and left it with the red text/red fill formatting:

	A	B	C	D	E	F	G	H	I
1					Hours Per Week				
2			15	20	25	30	35	40	
3		$ 15.00	$ 225.00	$ 300.00	$ 375.00	$ 450.00	$ 525.00	$ 600.00	
4		$ 20.00	$ 300.00	$ 400.00	$ 500.00	$ 600.00	$ 700.00	$ 800.00	
5		$ 25.00	$ 375.00	$ 500.00	$ 625.00	$ 750.00	$ 875.00	$1,000.00	
6		$ 30.00	$ 450.00	$ 600.00	$ 750.00	$ 900.00	$1,050.00	$1,200.00	

(Pay Rate label appears vertically in column A/B for rows 3–6)

Duplicate Values dialog box:

Format cells that contain:

Duplicate ⌄   values with   Light Red Fill with Dark Red Text ⌄

OK   Cancel

(Note that you can actually also use this choice to get Unique values by changing the dropdown in the Duplicate Values dialogue box.)

I want to point out one issue to you that makes this one not have a lot of value to me. And that's that it flags all duplicate values with the exact same formatting. So here we have duplicates of $300, $375, $450, $500, $600, and $750. But as far as the formatting is concerned, they're all treated the same.

Which if you did not want any duplicates at all in your data would probably be fine. As long as any cell is formatted with red, you know you still have duplicates.

But what if I wanted to look at my duplicates and figure out which one to keep? This is not a good data set for that, but let's say I had two entries for Students A, B, C, and D in a data table. This conditional formatting option will tell me I have duplicate entries for each of those students, but it doesn't let me easily isolate Student A's duplicate entries. Maybe Student A has three. How do I know that without doing more work? (I'd have to filter by Student A, I couldn't filter by format. And in a table like the one above, that's not an option, so I'd have to use Find to see how many entries I had for Student A.)

Okay. That's the duplicate value option, it may have some limited uses, just keep in mind its limitations.

What about the Text That Contains option? That one works fine, no big surprises.

I used it in the example below to flag all transactions in the Australian Amazon store in this report and it did just fine with it:

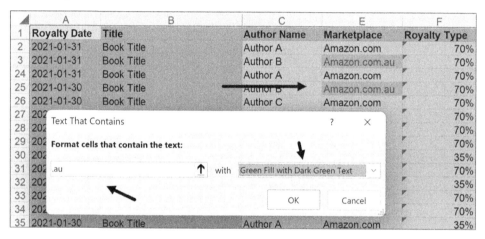

Note here that I'm still in that dialogue box but Excel is showing me what it will do to my data if I click OK. So if you put in criteria and realize that doing so flags entries you don't want to include, you can change it before you click OK. (Or Cancel.)

For example, if I had used "au" instead of ".au" that could have potentially captured other entries I didn't want.

Finally, let's look at the date one:

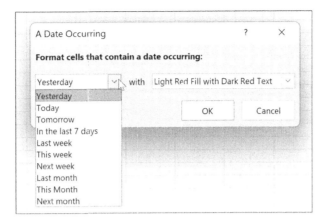

The choices are yesterday, today, tomorrow, last seven days, last week, this week, next week, last month, this month, and next month. I personally don't find this tremendously useful because I can't specify dates or criteria.

If you need one of those, great. But if you need some other set of dates to be flagged, conditional formatting using the Highlight Cells Rules option does not at this point in time give you that level of control. So, for example, "more than 30 days ago" is not an option. Nor is "between this date and that".

Also, the More Rules option doesn't give any additional choices. (This is a place they could make some useful improvements, hint, hint, so maybe that will change over time.)

Okay, next we have the Top/Bottom Rules.

Top/Bottom Rules

Here are the available quick options for that one:

They are labeled Top 10 Items, Top 10%, Bottom 10 Items, Bottom 10%, Above Average, and Below Average. But, when you click on the ten items or ten percent options, you can edit the number in the dialogue box like I have here for the top ten percent option, which I changed to the top twenty percent:

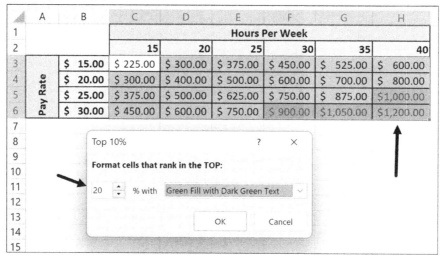

As for formatting, you have the same dropdown menu options as for the Highlight Cells Rules, including the Custom Format option at the bottom of the list.

There is also a More Rules option in the Top/Bottom Rules secondary dropdown menu which will open the New Formatting Rule dialogue box to the "Format only top or bottom ranked values" option, but it doesn't provide any additional options that aren't already listed.

Data Bars

Data bars is the one I mentioned above that I use in lieu of numbers so that I can see seasonal trends in my revenue, ad spend, and profit numbers. What this option does by default is it places a bar in each cell where the size of the bar in the cell is based upon the relative value of the amount in that cell compared to the other cells in the range.

That sounds horribly complicated, but it's not. Let's look at a few examples:

	A	B	C
1	**Example 1**	**Example 2**	**Example 3**
2	**1**	**10**	**1**
3	**2**	**20**	**100**
4	**3**	**30**	**1000**
5	**4**	**40**	**2500**
6	**5**	**50**	**10000**

Here I have three different columns of data. I have applied data bars to each column individually. (That's important, because that means that Column A's values are only being compared to the other values in Column A. Same for Columns B and C.)

Note the values in Column A are 1, 2, 3, 4, and 5. And that the values in Column B are 10, 20, 30, 40, and 50.

The relative relationships between the five values in each of those columns are identical even though the numbers themselves are different. Five is five times one, fifty is five times ten. Same relative relationship. And that's true for all five numbers.

Which is why the data bars you see in those cells are the same. The data bar in Row 2 is one-fifth the size of the data bar in Row 6 for those two columns.

But in Column C the data bars do not work like that, because the numbers I've provided there have a different relationship to one another. 1 is one-ten-thousandth of the final entry 10,000. That's why you can't even see its data bar. 2,500 is one-fourth of 10,000 which is why its data bar takes up one-fourth of its cell.

By default, when working with data bars, the largest value (Y) will have a data bar that takes up the entire cell. Every other value (X) will have a data bar that takes up X/Y portion of its cell. That's why in Columns A and B the data bars are the same size for each row despite the difference in the numeric values, and why each bar is 1/5 bigger than the bar in the row above.

The data bar menu choices are very basic:

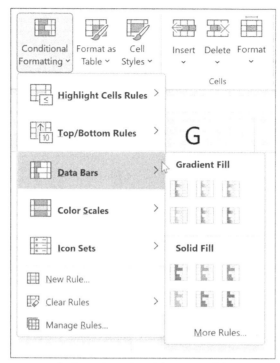

You can basically choose one of six colors in either a solid version (as I did above) or in a gradient version. The gradient shows within each cell. So each data bar shades from darker to lighter, however big that data bar is. Like so:

	A	B	C
1	Example 1	Example 2	Example 3
2	1	10	1
3	2	20	100
4	3	30	1000
5	4	40	2500
6	5	50	10000

Which means that choosing gradient here is just an aesthetic choice. The shading does not give additional information about relative value.

Where things can get interesting with data bars is if you click on that More Rules option and bring up the New Formatting Rule dialogue box. By default, data bars are applied as I described above where it looks at the actual values in the cells and then applies bars based on their relation to one another. But you can change that.

Here, for example, for the data bars in Column B I've set a specific range that is not based on the values in those cells. Now the data bars are applied based upon where a value falls between 0 and 100. That means for each cell the data bar size is determined by the value in that cell (X) divided by 100.

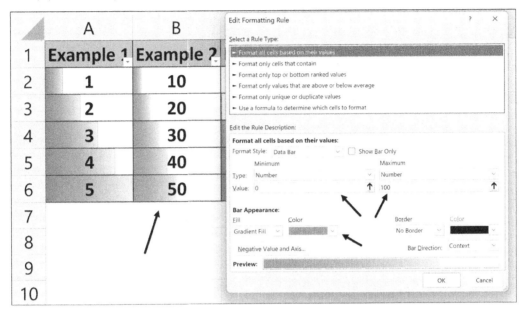

Now 50, our largest value, only generates a data bar that's half the size of the cell.

You can also see that I used the Color dropdown menu to choose a custom color other than one of the six default choices.

The other thing I want to point out to you is that little checkbox for "Show Bar Only". If you don't want to be distracted by the actual values, you can check that box and then you will not see the values in those cells. Like so:

	A	B	C
1	Example 1	Example 2	Example 3
2	1		1
3	2		100
4	3		1000
5	4		2500
6	5		10000

Just be careful on that one. Because, as I showed you at the beginning, data bars for 1, 2, 3, 4, and 5 are going to look identical to the data bars for 10, 20, 30, 40, and 50. So you lose that type of nuance when you hide the values behind the data bars.

Say, for example, these two columns represented sales performance for two sales reps. You'd think that Sales Rep A and Sales Rep B are performing the same, and in terms of percent increase per month they are, but you'd miss the fact that Rep B sells ten times as much as Rep A every month.

Okay. On to Color Scales.

Color Scales

Color scales is one I use a lot. It's the one I use to shade my revenue, ad spend, and profit and loss values per month.

What they do is color a cell a shade of a color or along a continuum of colors based upon the relative value in that cell compared to the values in the rest of the selected cells.

So, much like data bars except color-based. And, like data bars, the secondary menu for this one is color choices:

In this case you can choose green-yellow-red, red-yellow-green, green-white-red, red-white-green, blue-white-red, red-white-blue, white-red, red-white, green-white, white-green, green-yellow, and yellow-green.

I almost always use the More Rules option to choose a different color since red, green, and yellow tend to have set meanings of "bad", "good", and "okay". So I'll often use the color dropdown menu and change it so that my color for the lowest value is the lightest color in one of the provided color columns and the color for my highest value is one of the darkest colors in that same column. Like so:

Be careful on this one what colors you choose and what that implies. For example, if I go from gray to orange to brown, which of those colors is "good"? Which is "bad"?

If all you want is to distinguish values from one another, that's fine. But if you're trying to see the "best" results or the "worst" results, take that into consideration when choosing your colors.

Make sure the color you use supports what you're trying to display. At least in the United States, for example, you don't want to shade your "good" values red since red is generally considered "bad". Especially if the other end of the shading spectrum is green which is usually considered "good."

Also, if using a color like red or green, you may want to use multiple colors. Let's say -100 is good and 100 is bad but if it's all shades of red it makes it all look "bad" to one degree or another. Same with all green, it makes it all look "good" to one degree or another.

Two more things to point out here. We've been dealing with set values, but you can also have Excel apply color scales (or data bars) based upon percent, percentile, or a formula that you provide.

You also have the choice to customize to either a two-color scale or three-color scale by changing the Format Style dropdown.

Finally, if you do have color scales that use a really dark color and you want your values to show in the cell, consider formatting those cells using white text to make the entries more visible.

(You could do this by adding a second conditional formatting rule to that cell range that applies white text to cells with values in that upper range using a custom format and the Highlight Cells Rules. Or if the data is relatively stable, just format those cells with white text manually.)

Okay, next up, Icon Sets.

Icon Sets

Icon sets are much like color scales or data bars, except they show various icons next to the values. Here's the dropdown menu:

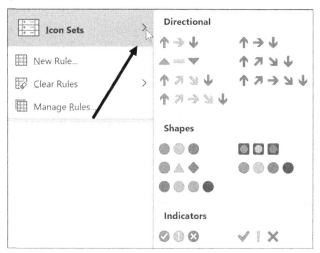

Here are some examples of those in action:

	A	B	C
1	**Example 1**	**Example 2**	**Example 3**
2	⬇ 1	⚫ 10	📊 1
3	⬇ 2	⚫ 20	📊 100
4	➡ 3	⚪ 30	📊 1000
5	⬆ 4	⚫ 40	📊 2500
6	⬆ 5	⚫ 50	📊 10000

As you can see there are choices that break your data into thirds, fourths, or even fifths, some of which also use color-coding. If you use these icons on your data, Excel will let you then filter your results by icon using the Filter By Color option:

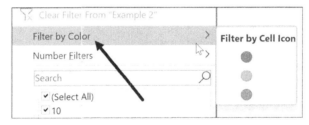

(This is also available if you're using color scales, but not for data bars.)

You can use the More Rules option to bring up the New Formatting Rule dialogue box and customize your icon sets. You can either use one of the same icon sets already shown or combine different elements of an icon set using the dropdown menu:

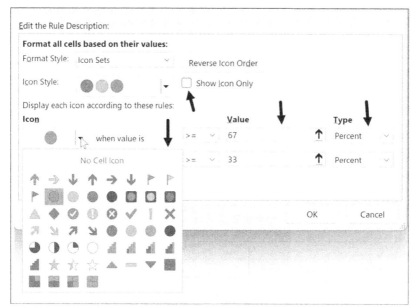

And you can set parameters as percent of the range, number, percentile, or as a formula. Here I've combined icons from three different icon sets and used absolute number values to apply the icons:

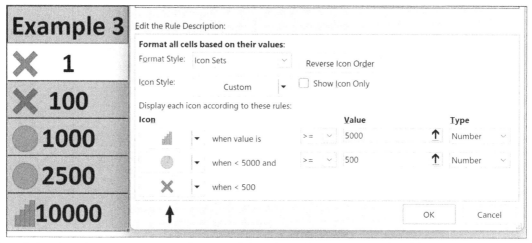

(Proof that just because you can do something doesn't mean you should.)

New Rule

If you just want to jump straight in to customizing a rule and don't want Excel to start you off with any sort of help, you can choose New Rule from the Conditional Formatting dropdown menu in the Styles section of the Home tab.

This will open the New Formatting Rule dialogue box set to the top option, "Format all cells based on their values" and then you can navigate from there.

In general, I wouldn't recommend this. Because as you've seen with the More Rules option on each of the secondary dropdown menus, going to one of those first starts you off on the right screen when you open the New Formatting Rule dialogue box.

In my opinion it's better to know the type of conditional formatting you want to apply and click on the More Rules option from that secondary dropdown menu instead.

The only exception to this might be the final option there, "Use a formula to determine which cells to format". Because if you're applying basic formatting to your cells using a formula (and not applying data bars, color scales, or icons), that may only be possible through this option and there's no quick shortcut to get there.

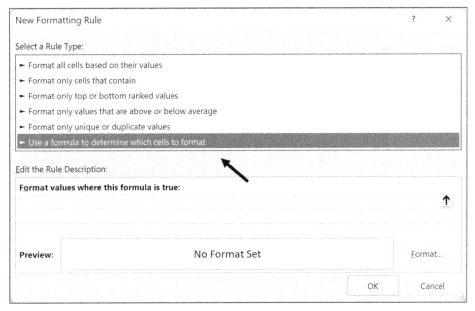

Using Formulas

Okay, so let's talk about using a formula. First, know that the help screen for conditional formatting has a very useful video on this if you want to reinforce what I say here or see another example.

To write a formula for conditional formatting, the formula must return a true or false value and start with an equals sign (which indicates that it's a formula).

For example, let's say that I want to flag those results in Column C where the value in Column B is greater. What you do is write your formula so that it returns a TRUE or FALSE value based upon the first cell in your selected range.

Here, for example, my selected cell range begins with Cell C2:

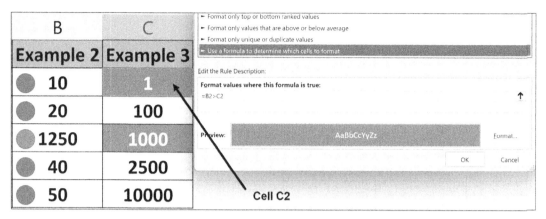

Cell C2

Which means the formula I write in the formula field in my New Formatting Rule dialogue box has to be written for that cell. (I've selected Cells C2 through C6 to apply the formatting, but the cell I write the formula for is Cell C2.)

The formula I wrote is

$$=B2>C2$$

That says, this is a formula (=), look at B2, is it greater than C2? If so, return a value of TRUE, which means format the cell. If not, return a value of FALSE and don't format the cell.

I had it apply a bright green fill and white text. But note that you can also use formulas for data bars, color scales, and icon sets.

The key with formulas is to write them so that they return a TRUE or FALSE result and to write them as if writing a formula for the top cell in the selected range.

Also, you can't reference values in an external workbook although you can reference a value in another worksheet.

Copy Conditional Formatting To New Data

There are a few more topics to cover, but before I forget this and because it's especially useful with dealing with formulas and conditional formatting, if you want to copy conditional formatting from one cell to another, you can use the Format Painter in the Clipboard section of the Home tab.

I just did this a moment ago and it worked like a charm, so hopefully the same is true for you. Click on the cell with the conditional formatting you want to copy, then click on the Format Painter image in the Clipboard, and then click on the cell(s) where you want to transfer that conditional formatting.

I was able to take the formula-based formatting we just created and copy that to Cell F8 with no issues using this approach.

Edit Rules

I will admit that I have been cheating a bit with some of the screenshots you've seen in this section. Because I couldn't show you the conditional formatting applied and the settings I'd applied at the same time using the New Formatting Rule dialogue box. I had to apply the formatting and then go edit the rule to get the dialogue box settings visible next to the formatted cells.

So how do you edit an existing conditional formatting rule? Go to the Conditional Formatting dropdown menu and choose Manage Rules from the bottom of the dropdown menu.

That will open the Conditional Formatting Rules Manager which will default to showing the rules applied to your current selection:

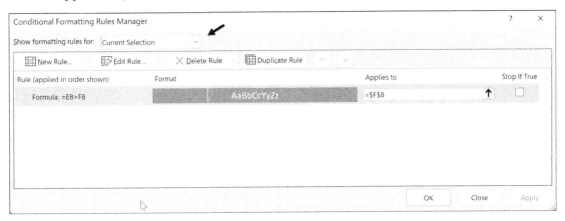

You can change that dropdown to the current worksheet or to any other worksheet in your workbook.

To edit an existing rule, click on the row for that rule and then click on Edit Rule. This will bring up the familiar-by-now dialogue box, but the top of the dialogue box will say that it's the Edit Formatting Rule dialogue box.

Make the changes you want to make and then click on OK. This will take you back to the Conditional Formatting Rules Manager dialogue box where you can either click OK or Apply to make your change. OK will close the dialogue box. Apply will apply the change but keep the dialogue box open.

I will sometimes edit my conditional formatting rules to extend the cell reference range by clicking into the box that lists the referenced cells and editing it. It's probably not the best method to use. But if you do it, do not use the arrow keys while in that box. It will start editing your cell reference range. You need to either click directly where you want to make your edit or backspace to delete the text until you get to that spot.

You can also use the arrow with a bar under it at the end of the listed cell range to select your cell range directly in the worksheet.

I used to have to do this because I would add more entries at the bottom of an existing set of data and the conditional formatting would not carry through to the new entries, but when I was writing this chapter it looks like maybe Excel now extends formatting automatically for you.

Delete Rule or Clear Formatting

If you want to delete a single conditional formatting rule, you can do so through the Manage Rules option in the Conditional Formatting dropdown menu. Click on Manage Rules, find the rule you want to delete, select it, and then click Delete Rule.

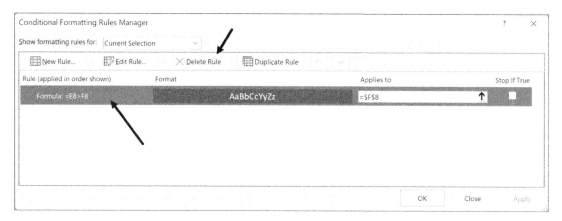

If you want to clear all conditional formatting from a cell or range of cells, though, I think that Quick Analysis option we discussed at the start is faster. Select your cell(s), click on the Quick Analysis icon in the bottom right corner, and then click on the Clear Format option.

There is also a menu option to clear rules from cells. Go to the Conditional Formatting dropdown menu, go down to Clear Rules, and then choose either Clear Rules from Selected Cells or Clear Rules from Entire Worksheet.

(We're going to cover conditional formatting of pivot tables in the pivot table section, but there's an option for that there as well.)

Find Conditional Formatting

If you use the Manage Rules option and choose to look at the current worksheet, that's going to show you all of the rules in that worksheet and which cells they apply to.

But according to Excel, you can also use the Find option to find conditional formatting.

Go to the Editing section of the Home tab, click on the dropdown arrow for Find & Select, and then choose Conditional Formatting from there:

What that does is selects every cell in the worksheet that has conditional formatting applied. They're shaded gray and if you choose to remove conditional formatting from selected cells it will remove it from all of the cells in that worksheet that have conditional formatting applied.

If you want to just find a specific type of conditional formatting, click on a cell that has that type of formatting applied, and then go to the Find & Select option and choose Go To Special. In the dialogue box that appears, click on Conditional Formats, and then choose Same under Data Validation. That will highlight all of the cells that have that specific conditional formatting.

I did have one situation where it did not work where I had used the Format Painter to transfer a formula-based conditional format to a cell that was not in the same column, but otherwise I was able to get it to work.

Multiple Rules

One final thought. It is possible, as I alluded to before when talking about formatting cells with white text if the fill color on that cell is dark, to apply more than one type of conditional formatting to the same cell or range of cells.

Be careful if you do this that the formatting doesn't conflict, because one format may overwrite the other.

There is a "Stop if True" checkbox you can click for a rule to make sure that if there are multiple rules that if one is met no more conditional formatting is applied.

Also, you can change the order of the rules, by using the Manage Rules option to see all rules and then moving a rule above or below the others to get them to apply in the "correct" order. I find that I sometimes just have to experiment a bit to get the result I want.

And since I haven't said it yet in this book, remember that Ctrl + Z, Undo, is your friend. If you do something that looks bad, undo it, and try again.

Insert Symbols

That was a lot to cover, so let's step back and discuss a few much simpler things you can do in Excel. I'll start with how to insert a symbol into a cell.

This isn't going to come up often, but let's say you're using text in your worksheet and find yourself needing to insert the copyright symbol, ©.

The easiest way to do that, assuming you haven't changed your settings to prevent it, is to just type (c) in the cell. When you then hit the space bar to move forward that will convert into the copyright symbol.

Excel has a number of these shortcuts pre-programmed. You can see them if you go to the File tab and then click on Options at the bottom of the screen to open the Excel Options dialogue box. Go to the Proofing section on the left-hand side and then click on AutoCorrect Options to open the AutoCorrect Options dialogue box:

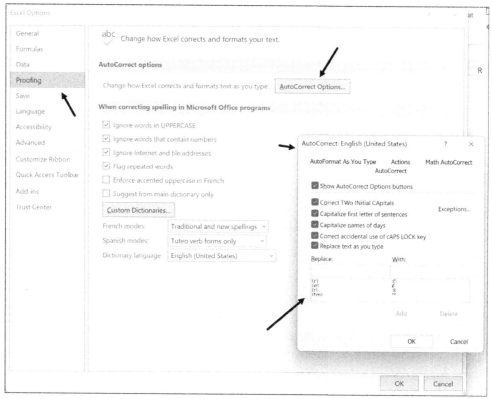

It's a little hard to see in that screenshot, but there are shortcuts listed for copyright, Euro, registered trademark, and trademark. If you click over to the Math AutoCorrect tab you'll see that there are many more text to symbol options listed there.

If you don't like one of the autocorrect options you can delete it. For example, I did a lot of regulatory work at one point in time and was far more likely to be referring to 3110(c) than I was to need the copyright symbol. So one of the first things I would do when I upgraded to a new version of Word or Excel was track that one down and delete it.

You can also add a shortcut to that list if there's a symbol you use often. In the AutoCorrect Options dialogue box, type the shortcut text you want to use in the Replace field, and then paste in the symbol you want in the With field. Click Add and then OK.

(I'll show you in a moment how to insert a symbol without using a shortcut so that you can insert that symbol and copy it for use in creating your shortcut.)

Just think it through before you create a shortcut. I have a program where I mainly do formatting and have shortcuts set up for applying formatting to my text using Shift + 1, Shift + 2, and Shift + 3. They're great to use, because they're right there, but each time I need an exclamation mark, an at sign, or a pound sign, I have a problem. It's worth it to me in that program because I need the formats more than I need those three symbols, but every once in a while it catches me out.

To insert a symbol without using a shortcut, click into the location where you want to insert that symbol—so a blank cell or within the text that's already in a cell. Go to the Insert tab and at the far right end there should be an image for Symbols with a dropdown arrow. Click on that and choose Symbol from the dropdown menu.

That will open the Symbol dialogue box:

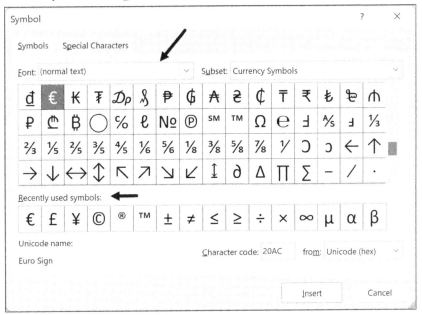

A few key things to point out here. At the top is a dropdown menu for Font and Subset. In the screenshot above the font is (normal text) and the subset is Currency Symbols.

Below that are four rows of symbols related to that font and subset.

You can either change the font or subset using the dropdown menus or you can use the scroll bar on the right-hand side of those symbols to move through all of your symbols.

Below the symbols related to the font and subset is a row of "recently used symbols".

I haven't used any symbols in Excel yet, so this is Excel's default list: some currency symbols, some copyright and trademark symbols, and then some mathematical symbols.

The math symbols you see are text, not something to use to perform mathematical calculations. You use an asterisk for multiplication in an Excel formula, not an x, for example.

Note also that there is another tab you can click on at the top of the dialogue box for Special Characters. These are mostly writing-related. So various types of dashes, hyphens, spaces, quotes, etc.

If you see the symbol you want, double-click on it to insert it in your cell. If that's all you needed, click Close or the X in the top right corner to close the dialogue box. If you need another symbol, go find it and insert it.

If the symbol you want is not visible, then you'll need to use the scroll bar on the side or use the Font or Subset dropdown menus to get to the font you want.

Often the Wingdings fonts include images so if that's the sort of thing you need, look there first:

I have some custom fonts that also include images. Just be aware that if you use a font other users don't have they may not be able to see that "symbol" as an image. Also, if you use Wingdings or another font like that, be very careful about changing your font after you do so.

Here, for example, in Cell A1 I have the Euro symbol inserted using the default (normal text) menu that was available when I opened the Symbols dialogue box. Next to that is a yin yang symbol I inserted from the Wingdings font and then a stylistic little symbol I also inserted from there as well.

You can see in the formula bar that the yin yang symbol is actually a left bracket ([ ) and that the stylistic symbol has no associated character. It takes up a space in that formula bar, but there's nothing to see there.

I copied the contents of Cell A1 to Cell A2 and applied the Arial font to the contents. You can see that the Euro symbol is still a Euro symbol, although it has changed to reflect the applied font. But because we're no longer using the Wingdings font in Cell A2, the yin yang symbol became a left bracket and the stylistic symbol is gone. (It will come back, though if I change the font for that cell to Wingdings. Same with the yin yang symbol. But if I do that, the Euro symbol changes to a zero in a circle.)

Most symbols are tied in to the chosen font. So if you use them, have your font established before you start inserting them, just to be safe. The ones that are shown under the (normal text) section probably have an equivalent version in most fonts, but I'd still double-check them after changing the font.

Once inserted into your worksheet a symbol can be formatted color- and size-wise like any other text.

Insert Equations

You may have noticed that in that same dropdown menu for symbols there was also an option for Equation:

Click on that option and you'll see some pre-formatted equations such as the two above for area of a circle and binomial theorem.

   If you click on one of these options, it will insert as a text box. It is not inserting the equation into a cell in your worksheet. It inserts on top of the worksheet and can be moved around within the worksheet by clicking and dragging when your cursor looks like four arrows, one pointing in each direction.

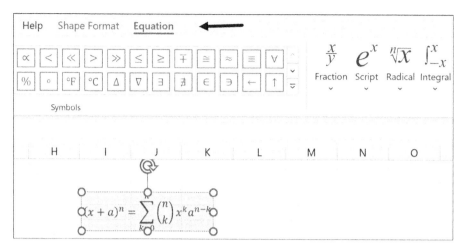

Above you can see that I inserted the binomial theorem equation and that it's sitting on top of my cells, it's not part of any of them. This is a visual presentation of a formula not to help you build a function that uses that formula.

When you insert an equation into your worksheet, Excel will display two new tab options, Shape Format and Equation. These will be visible at any time that you have the equation selected and will not be visible at other times.

I could use the Equation tab options to insert additional symbols to help build out the formula from here.

You can't see the full section, but on the right-hand side are more options grouped by category (Fraction, Script, Radical, Integral, etc.) where there are dropdown menus and you can select common notation for each of those categories.

On the left-hand side of the Equation tab are three options for how to format the equation: Professional, Linear, and Normal Text. The default format is Professional which uses italics for letters like n unlike the Normal Text option which does not. The Linear option writes the entire formula on a single line. So (x+a) to the nth power becomes (x+a)^n, for example.

The Shape Format tab is where you can change the color and style of the text of the equation or the border around the text. (Although for the text the normal text formatting options on the Home tab will also work as long as you select the text first.)

I'm not going to dive in any deeper on this, because I don't think many people will need it, I just wanted to mention it because it was there and you might have been curious.

I'll just close with a reminder that Excel treats these equations not as text, but as shapes. They will not behave like normal cells and text do.

Insert Illustrations

I don't want to cover this one in detail either, but I feel I have to at least mention it because more people are using illustrations in Excel and if you come across one like I did the other day, you need to know how to deal with them.

In that same Insert tab, on the left-hand side is an option for Illustrations. If you click on the dropdown arrow you'll see a number of choices, including Pictures, Shapes, Icons, 3D Models, SmartArt, and Screenshots.

Here I've clicked on the dropdown arrow for Shapes and you can see the beginning of what is a very large dropdown menu of shapes that can be inserted into an Excel worksheet:

For Pictures, Icons, and 3D Models, when you make your selection and click on Insert it will automatically insert on top of the worksheet.

For Shapes, click on one of those options and then click and drag on the worksheet to create the shape.

For SmartArt, after you choose your SmartArt it will insert a template on your worksheet along with a dialogue box where you can input the values you want to use.

All of these are inserted on top of the worksheet, not embedded in an individual cell in the worksheet. You can click and drag them around (when the cursor has arrows pointing in four directions).

You can also resize them by clicking on them and then clicking and dragging from one of the white circles in the corners or around the perimeter. Be careful about scale because if you click from one of the sides then only the height or only the width will adjust, but not both.

You can also resize using the special Format tab which will appear for that object. (The names are slightly different for each tab, but they all have Format in them and will appear to the right of the Help tab when you click on the object.) Size is at the far right side on each tab. Input the numeric values you want there.

That Format tab is also where you can specify colors, borders, etc. and where you can dictate which of multiple objects is in front or in back if they happen to overlap.

I could spend a good forty pages on this and do cover SmartArt and objects in far more detail in the PowerPoint books, but most of you will not need it in Excel. So all I'm going to tell you here is that if you see text in a worksheet that doesn't seem to be part of a cell, it's likely from a shape someone has inserted into that worksheet. And if you need to remove it (like I recently did with Amazon's attribution tracking workbook), click on the object and use Delete.

Okay. On to our next big topic, Charts.

Charts – Basics and Types

Charts are a great way to visualize data. Sometimes numbers can be overwhelming, but a quick picture based on those numbers makes trends and patterns very clear.

Data Format

First things first, you need to format your data so that Excel can use it to create a chart.

(We'll talk about pivot tables and pivot charts later. If you work with those the pivot table basically already does this for you and then Excel knows how to build charts off of it, but I wanted to cover charts first before we have that conversation.)

For most chart types you want data labels across the top and data labels down the side, but no grand totals or sub-totals or sub-headers. Like this:

	January-2020	February-2020	April-2020	May-2020	June-2020	July-2020	August-2020	Total
Author A	$23.60	$74.26	$262.40	$296.36	$266.15	$250.00	$322.00	**$1,494.77**
Author B	$17.13	$6.88	$95.68	$3.44	$6.88	$5.59	$121.00	**$256.60**
Author C	$8.44	$6.01	$61.76	$8.98	$5.34	$1.47	$681.81	**$773.80**
Author D	$8.63	$0.52	$13.86	$22.08	$50.85	$128.46	$61.22	**$285.62**
Author E	$3.38	$0.07	$2.74	$3.47	$16.05	$11.24	$42.12	**$79.07**
Author F	$1.69	$0.06	$1.29	$1.33	$3.78	$7.14	$40.84	**$56.12**

(I usually do not include any sort of label in that top left corner, but just now when I left one there it still worked. Note this is randomly-generated data not real sales data.)

Which data label goes across the top versus down the side will impact the default chart that Excel tries to build when you choose your chart type, but there's an option to flip those if it's not how you want it in the chart, so don't worry too much about that.

If you do happen to have grand totals or labels like I do here with the Total Column, that's okay, but you'll want to select only the cells with the data and labels you want to include in your chart.

It is important that you format the data in the table you're going to use before you create your chart. I will often create charts that include a data table below the chart and when I do that the formatting of those values is directly sourced from the original data table.

So, for example, when I'm going to include a data table below my chart, I format my currency values to not have any decimal places, because it takes up too much space and that level of detail is not necessary.

Create a Chart

To create a chart, select the data you want to use for the chart and then go to the Charts section of the Insert tab and click on the dropdown for the chart type you want.

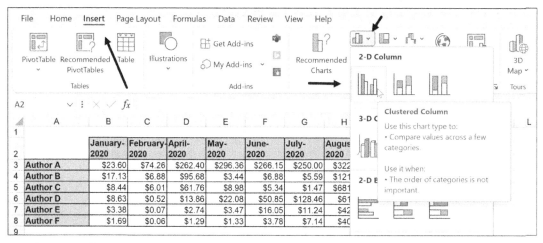

From there you'll see a list of available choices. If you hold your mouse over each one, Excel will tell you more about that specific type of chart (as you can see above for Clustered Column).

It will also create and show you the chart, but not actually insert it. If you move your mouse, the chart will disappear.

When you find the chart option you want, simply click on it and that chart will then be officially inserted into your worksheet and remain there after you move your mouse away. Charts work like equations and illustrations so are inserted on top of your worksheet, not as part of a cell. Like this:

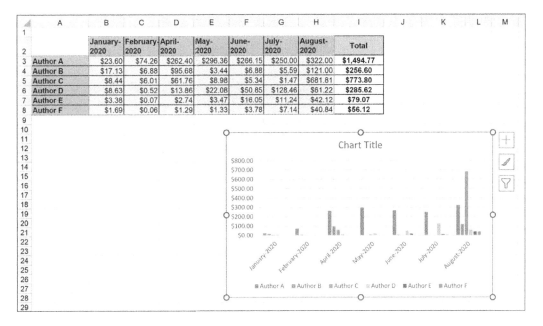

The chart is going to stay in that worksheet unless you deliberately move it, but it's on top of the cells, not embedded in them, so you can left-click and drag to move it around in the workspace without the cells being impacted.

Another option for inserting a chart is to select your data, go to the Insert tab, and then click on Recommended Charts instead. This will open the Insert Chart dialogue box and will show some recommended charts based on your data.

You can also click over to All Charts and click through there to see how your data will look with each chart type like I've done here:

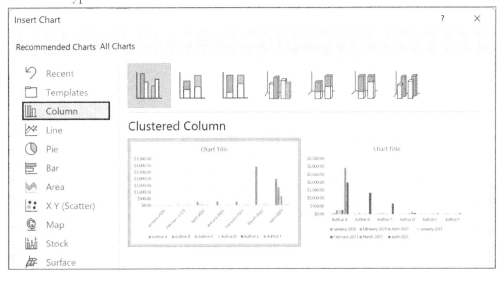

Once you find a chart you like, click on it and then click OK and it will insert.

Another option for inserting a chart is to use the Quick Analysis option. Select your data and then click on the quick analysis icon in the bottom right corner and go to Charts and you'll see some basic options there:

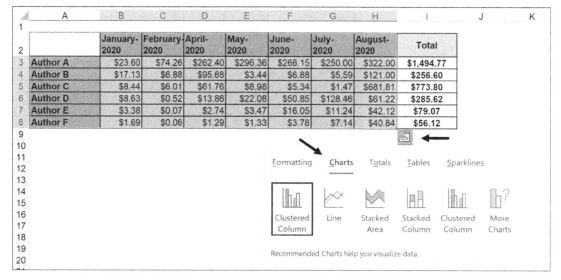

Click on any of those chart options and a chart of that type will immediately be inserted into your worksheet. Clicking on More Charts opens the Insert Chart dialogue box.

* * *

It is possible to create a chart using data that is not touching.

For example, I will sometimes have a chart like the one above that also has a totals column at the end, and want to create a chart using just that totals column. But I also need the first column to know what the values represent.

In that case, use Ctrl to select your two cell ranges, like I have here with Column A and Column I:

	January-2020	February-2020	April-2020	May-2020	June-2020	July-2020	August-2020	Total
Author A	$23.60	$74.26	$262.40	$296.36	$266.15	$250.00	$322.00	$1,494.77
Author B	$17.13	$6.88	$95.68	$3.44	$6.88	$5.59	$121.00	$256.60
Author C	$8.44	$6.01	$61.76	$8.98	$5.34	$1.47	$681.81	$773.80
Author D	$8.63	$0.52	$13.86	$22.08	$50.85	$128.46	$61.22	$285.62
Author E	$3.38	$0.07	$2.74	$3.47	$16.05	$11.24	$42.12	$79.07
Author F	$1.69	$0.06	$1.29	$1.33	$3.78	$7.14	$40.84	$56.12

Selected Data

Just make sure that your selected ranges are the same size. I've selected Cell A2 here even though it has no data in it because I have that Total label in Cell I2 that I want to include. After that it's the same process of going to the Insert tab and making a choice. (I couldn't see the Quick Analysis option when the data I selected was not contiguous, but maybe that will change in the future.)

Which Chart

That was how to insert charts, but a big part of working with charts is figuring out which one to use. There are a few things to consider when looking at your data and making this choice. We'll walk through the type of questions you can ask yourself first and then we'll dig in and look at examples of each of the chart types mentioned.

So ask yourself…

Is there a time component to the data? For example, are you looking at sales across the months of a year?

I will, for example, use charts to look at sales for 13 months for each author name, series name, and title I publish to see if those sales are steady, increasing, or decreasing and to also compare to the same time period one year before.

For that sort of scenario, something like a bar or column chart or even a line chart is a good option. Each of those lets you visually see the changes across time periods.

Bar and column charts are better for when you have multiple variables you want to chart, like my analysis of the performance of multiple titles over the course of a year. Line charts work better with a single variable. (Although, there is a type of chart related to line charts, the area chart, that you can use for multiple variables, but at that point you're not working with a straight line, you're working with a shaded area. We'll get back to this.)

Are you instead looking to see what share of the whole each component represents? For example, at year-end I want to see what percentage of my total sales each series represented for that year. It's a snapshot of that year, I'm not looking at trends over time.

In that case something like a pie chart or doughnut chart is a good choice.

Are you trying to find a relationship between different variables? For example, how does the value of X impact the value of Y?

A scatter plot is a good choice for that one. (Excel calls them scatter charts.) You can also use a bubble chart.

Are you trying to see the distribution of a series of results. So, what's the average outcome given the data you have? In that case, a histogram can be a good choice.

There are a number of other chart types that Excel offers, but those are the ones I'm going to cover in this book. If you're curious or you need a different chart type, you can see all of them in the All Charts tab of the Insert Chart dialogue box:

Click through to see how each one will look with your data. Some of the options require a third data component or a specific format. When that's the case they won't show a preview but will instead tell you what kind of data they need. (See Stock as a good example of this.)

If you use one of those other chart types, this is a good place to open Excel's Help related to that chart and read it so you know any quirks the chart type might have. Hopefully when we're done with this discussion you'll have a solid foundation for how to insert and format any chart, but the key issue for each chart type is generally going to be making sure that you've formatted your data properly.

Okay, then. Let's now discuss our chosen chart types in more detail.

Column and Bar Charts

Column and bar charts are basically the same thing. The main difference is whether the bars are vertical (columns) or horizontal (bars.)

In the Insert Chart dialogue box they are currently listed separately, but in the Charts section of the Insert tab they are currently combined under the top leftmost choice. Here are your options:

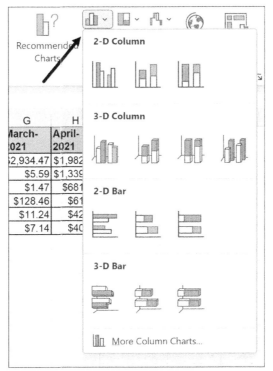

That More Column Charts choice does not in fact give you more choices, it just takes you to the Insert Chart dialogue box and gives you the same options you can see here.

The 3D options work the same as the 2D options, it's just a matter of whether you want three dimensionality or not. Since they're basically the same, I'm just going to cover your 2D choices in that first and third row.

Hold your mouse over the top of each of the three 2D choices for column or bar charts in that dropdown and you'll see that they are named clustered, stacked, and 100% stacked, respectively.

The icons for each one try to give a feel for what they look like, but we'll look at actual examples below.

Clustered column or bar charts take the results for each variable and place them side-by-side for each time period or category. For example, in the charts below we have author income for each month for six authors with a column or bar for each author for each time period, where the size of the column or bar is based on the dollar-value of the sales for that author for that time period relative to all dollar values in the data set.

Clustered column charts can get very busy very fast so they're not the best choice when you have a large number of variables if you're also looking at a large number of time periods or categories.

Stacked column or bar charts have one column or bar per time period or category. The overall size of the column or bar for each period or category is based on the total for all variables for the period and relative to the totals for the other periods or categories. There are separate colored or shaded sections of each column or bar for each variable to show the share of the total for that variable.

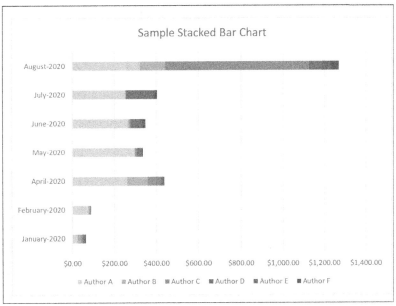

It's basically taking the individual columns or bars from a clustered chart and stacking them on top of each other.

Stacked charts are good for seeing trends over time for total performance. We can see here, for example, that August 2020 was much better than the prior months. And that January/February 2020 were much lower than the other months.

But stacked charts make it harder to see trends for the individual components that make up that whole. I can still see how Author A was dominant in most months and how Author C did really well in August 2020, but the clustered chart is better for seeing those individual-level trends.

The last bar or column chart type is the 100% stacked chart. The size of the column or bar for each time period or category is always the same, because it's always 100% of the total for that period or category.

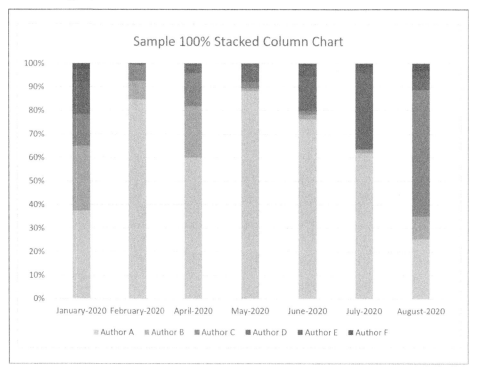

Each bar or column will be colored or shaded in sections to show the percent of the whole for each variable.

With a 100% stacked chart you lose the relative difference in actual results between time periods. Above you can see change in percentage of the whole better—we can really see that Author A dominated in all time periods—but you can't see that the first time period only had sales of $63 and the last time period had sales of $1269.

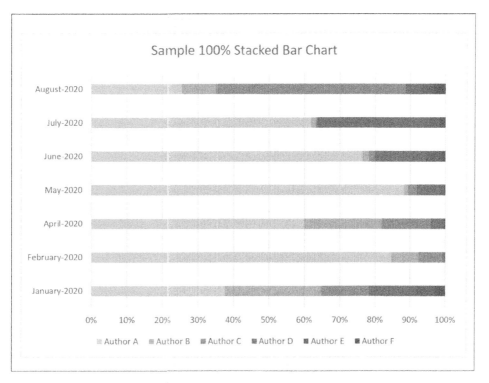

The risk with this one is that a column for $10, $40, and $50 will look the same as a column for $10,000, $40,000, and $50,000. So, if the actual amount earned in a period matters, don't rely on the 100% stacked chart for your analysis.

(One final note here, if there is a component that's a significant outlier, it can sometimes help to remove that component from the analysis so that you can better see the detail for the others. I will often drop my top-selling author or series name from my analysis to better see the results for my other authors and series.)

Pie or Doughnut Chart

As mentioned above, a pie or doughnut chart is good for a snapshot analysis where you want to see how much each variable represents of the whole. These choices are available on the left-hand side, bottom row in the Charts section of the Insert tab. Here are your choices:

Once again, the More Pie Charts option does not actually give you more choices and I'm skipping the 3D option which has a 2D counterpart.

The data for a pie or doughnut chart is a set of labels and then a set of values, so just two columns.

Here's a basic pie chart and doughnut chart of the same data:

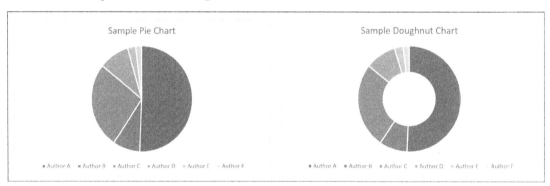

As you can see, the doughnut chart is just a hollowed-out version of the pie chart.

Both clearly show that for this data Authors A and C dominated the total share with Author A representing about half of all sales.

Those are the two main options and the ones I recommend using, but pie charts has two more options available, pie of pie and bar of pie.

These can be used to call out smaller values so that they're better visualized. BUT, if a reader is not used to seeing a chart like that, it can lead to some real confusion, in my opinion.

Let's look at the pie of pie chart for this same data to see what I'm talking about:

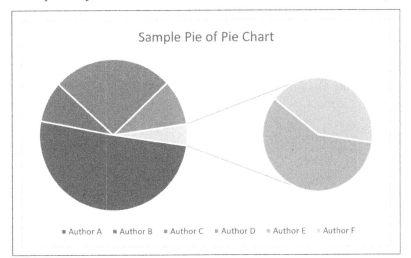

If I look at this chart without knowing how it works, I think that Author A is a big chunk of things, but then I turn to Author E in the other pie chart.

And what this is really doing is saying, "See that light blue slice of the left-hand pie? The *smallest* slice? Well that's actually two authors combined. And if we look at just those two authors in a separate pie chart, Author E has a bigger share of that small blue slice than Author F."

That right-hand pie chart that is so visible only represents 5% of the total sales. But because it gets called out this way it feels instinctively like it's a bigger share of things.

That's why if I am ever going to use one of these, I prefer the bar of pie chart, which looks like this:

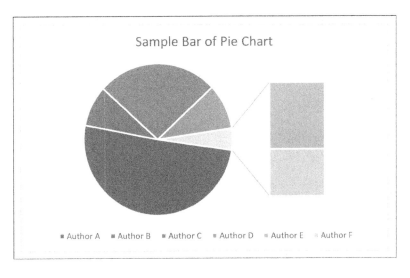

At least using a bar chart for the second chart makes it clear these are not apples to apples.

It still for me calls too much attention to those smallest values. If that slice were thirty different variables so that none of them dominated the bar chart on the right-hand side (and it's really a column, isn't it?) that might work.

But as is, with this data, I'm not a fan of using either of those charts to present this data. I'm sure they exist because there are circumstances where they make sense to use, but just be careful. Evaluate where a reader's eye might go and how they might interpret the image and whether that properly conveys the data. If it doesn't, don't use it.

Okay, now on to line and area charts.

Line and Area Charts

Line and area charts are the first chart type shown in the second row of choices in the Charts section of the Insert tab.

Once more we have 2D and 3D choices. And once more the More Choices option doesn't really give you more choices. The Insert Charts dialogue box has the choices you see here split between Line and Area charts.

Be sure here, and really with any data that has a time component to it, that your data is sorted in order. It can't be randomly listed in your data table.

I want to start by looking at the first option there which is the basic Line chart:

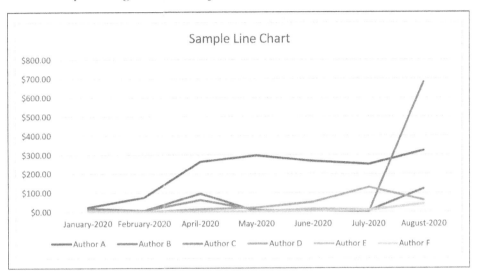

You can see here that very clear spike from Author C in August 2020. And you can see how Author A went up at the start and then plateaued at a level above the rest for most of the period.

Line charts are good for seeing a linear trend across time periods or categories. But they are not good for situations where you only have one or two data points. If I had a new author start selling in August 2020 there'd be no line to draw.

Here I've dropped Author C to better see the trend for the other authors and also changed the chart type to Line With Markers:

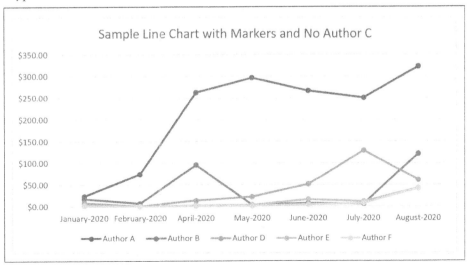

The line chart with markers option is the fourth listed choice. (It used to be that in older versions of Excel this lined up nicely so it was the first option on the second row, but that's no longer the case. Just think of it as the first of the options that shows markers, those dots on the line that represent specific data points.)

Using a line chart that includes markers for each data point can sometimes be helpful because it better shows where there's an actual data point versus where it's just a line connecting two points. The more markers between two points, the more faith you can have that the data actually followed that path.

Here, for example, is the data we've seen already for Authors A, B, and C for each month from January to August 2020 in the left-hand chart. In the right-hand chart we just have the data for January and for August.

For Author A, I have more faith that the change in earnings from January to August followed a steady pattern given the number of results in the first chart because there are six data points charting that rise versus just one in the second chart.

We can also see here how the second chart with just a beginning and an ending observation hides how Author C basically didn't perform at all until the final time period.

Basically, the more data, the better, and markers can be an indicator of how much data there was.

Those are the two line charts I recommend because they are what people traditionally expect of line charts. Each line is showing the values for that line and is separate from the other lines.

The other line chart options shown there are stacked and 100% stacked line charts. They act like the stacked and 100% stacked bar and column charts, meaning the lines are building upon one another to reach a total value for the period or to reach 100% for each period. But it's just not intuitive to most users that that's what they're seeing, so I don't recommend using them.

Here's the stacked line chart for this data, for example:

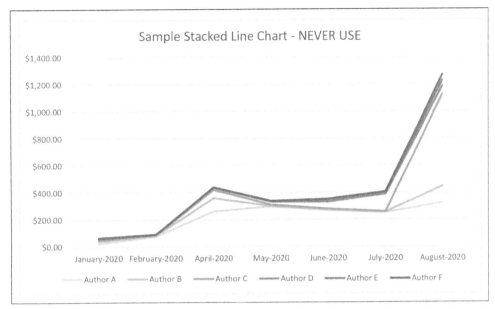

See what I mean? You just automatically assume that those lines are the results for each Author because that's how we're used to interpreting lines on charts. Or at least *I* do.

Area charts fix this issue. You've probably seen one or two over the last couple years, because they're used often with epidemiological data.

Here are the two area charts I recommend using applied to this data. The first is the Stacked Area chart:

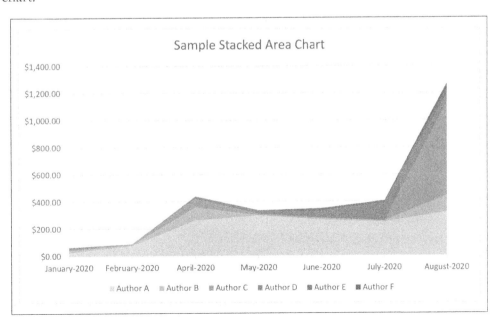

See how filling in the space between the lines gives the overall image cohesion? You can more readily understand that the various filled-in areas are adding up to something instead of representing separate results when the spaces between the lines are filled in.

The second is the 100% stacked area chart:

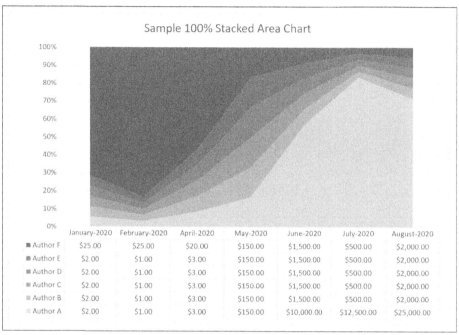

	January-2020	February-2020	April-2020	May-2020	June-2020	July-2020	August-2020
■ Author F	$25.00	$25.00	$20.00	$150.00	$1,500.00	$500.00	$2,000.00
■ Author E	$2.00	$1.00	$3.00	$150.00	$1,500.00	$500.00	$2,000.00
■ Author D	$2.00	$1.00	$3.00	$150.00	$1,500.00	$500.00	$2,000.00
■ Author C	$2.00	$1.00	$3.00	$150.00	$1,500.00	$500.00	$2,000.00
■ Author B	$2.00	$1.00	$3.00	$150.00	$1,500.00	$500.00	$2,000.00
■ Author A	$2.00	$1.00	$3.00	$150.00	$10,000.00	$12,500.00	$25,000.00

Be careful with the 100% stacked option, because it can give a misleading impression of the overall share of the results across time as you can see with the data I created for use in this one.

If you just look at the chart without the data, you would think that Author F and Author A just switched places. One was dominant early and then the other took over, but they basically had equal shares overall.

Which is true percentage-wise. Early on Author F was doing 2.5 times what all the other authors were doing combined. And at the end Author A was doing the same.

But what you'd completely miss from this chart (without the data table included) is that Author F made a grand total of $4,220 for the period covered by the chart and Author A made $47,656. Author A made *ten times* more than Author F, but that's completely hidden when you present the data using a 100% stacked area chart.

As a matter of fact, Author F who looks so great in this chart only earned $64 more than Authors B, C, D, and E.

Not obvious from what we see here because it's showing % share for each time period. The problem is that the use of a shaded area that crosses time periods makes the data feel connected when it's really not. At least not in that way.

The 100% stacked bar and column charts don't have this issue because each column or bar is discrete so they do a better job of reminding a viewer that the percentages are for that time period or category only.

Hope that makes sense. Basically, if you have wide swings in your actual results between time periods, do not use the 100% Stacked Area chart. It's misleading.

Okay, then. On to scatter plots.

Scatter and Bubble Plots

Scatter plots take two inputs and plot them on a grid to make a data point. A scatter plot can connect those data points to see if there's some sort of relationship between the two inputs, but it doesn't have to.

The scatter plot dropdown is the last one, on the bottom row, next to pie charts.

There are five options:

The first one just plots the points. The other options allow you to add either a smoothed line or a straight line that connects the points. The line can either show markers for the data points or not.

Here is a small data table with the data points plotted but not connected.

You can see that there's probably a relationship there, right? When one value goes up, so does the other. It's not perfectly linear, but it's there. (I created it so I know it's there.)

Now, here's the tricky thing with scatter plots. If I add a line connecting my data points Excel will draw that line by connecting the first point to the second point to the third point and on and on.

Here I used the smooth line option with markers:

That's a hot mess, isn't it? Why?

Because while there is a relationship between Value A and Value B, it's one that's independent of the order in which the observations were made.

If I sort my data by value, now we see it:

The data points didn't change. It's just the order in which they were connected that changed.

Whether you should sort the data in your plot like I just did or not is going to depend on what the data is and why it was in that order.

You can also plot multiple sets of data in the same scatter plot. The first column of data will drive the values on the x axis (the bottom) and then any other columns of data will be plotted against the y axis (the side).

Here, for example, I have three columns of data (Columns B, C, and D) plotted against the values in Column A.

You don't have to use lines when you do this, the data points for each column will have their own color, but I recommend it. It makes it easier to see which points belong to each column.

Above you can see that there is a relationship between the values in Column A and the values in Columns B, C, and D, but that that relationship is not the same. Here I've edited the values for Column C so there is no clear linear, quadratic, or binomial relationship:

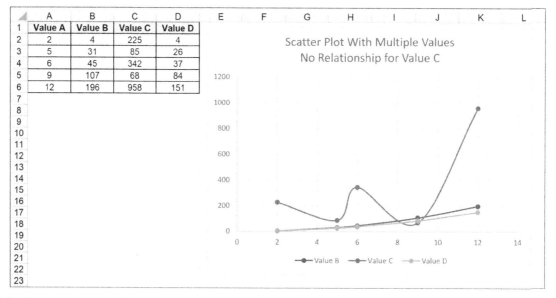

The line goes up and down and not in any apparent pattern.

In the same dropdown as scatter plots, you can also see bubble plots. A bubble plot takes two points and plots them against each other and then it takes one more piece of information and uses that to determine the size of the data point so you end up with three pieces of information shown for each data point.

Often you'll see this with country GDP, for example. So the original plot is spending versus population but then the size of the bubble is the overall "wealth" of the country. Or percent of population that adopted some health measure versus an outcome for that measure with the size of each data point showing per capita income. That sort of thing.

Here is a basic example, using the same data as our original scatter plot, but now with a number of observations column added to dictate the bubble size.

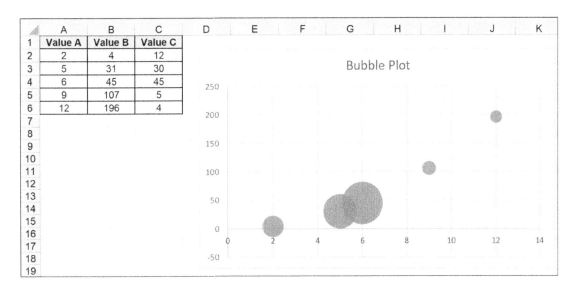

	A	B	C
1	Value A	Value B	Value C
2	2	4	12
3	5	31	30
4	6	45	45
5	9	107	5
6	12	196	4

This lets us see that the majority of the data is centered around two values for A, 5 and 6, which makes me less confident that the apparent pattern in this data exists since the data that is on the far left and on the far right is much less robust. (One outlier data point can sometimes skew your data in weird ways.) But there's still a handful of observations for each data point so it probably does exist. The bubble chart just lets me know to be more cautious with values for A that are further away from 5 or 6.

Okay. That was scatter and bubble plots. I used to use them a lot in physics class and economics, but one I actually use for my writing is the histogram. So let's talk about that one next.

Histogram

The histogram chart was a recent addition to Excel. It lets you take your data and create buckets of observations that are close in value and then plots a count of how many observations are in each bucket.

So instead of treating 31, 32, 33, and 34 as separate values, it might group those all into a 30 to 40 bucket. This can be nice because it removes the noise in your data and lets you better see any patterns.

The histogram option is in the middle of the chart choices and requires one column of values. Here I've created a histogram from randomly generated values between 0 and 100.

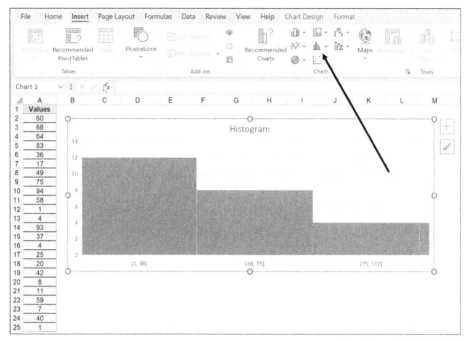

The histogram by default is going to look at the values that you give it and come up with the buckets it places those values into. In this case it used three buckets, 1 to 38, 38 to 75, and 75 to 112.

The height of each bar is based on the number of values that fall into that bucket. You can see that right now the 1 to 38 bucket contains the most values with 12 observations.

You can manually choose how many buckets to use and how wide they are in the formatting task pane (which we'll discuss in detail shortly.) For a histogram this is under Horizontal Axis, Axis Options, and then the Axis Options section. Here I've changed the number of bins (buckets) to ten and capped the histogram between 0 and 100.

As you can see it definitely impacts where we think most results will fall. Also, interestingly enough because I know how this data was created, we clearly don't have enough data points yet to see the true pattern in this data.

I added more observations and plotted again:

This is far closer to the true data pattern behind these values but still not quite there. Which is a reminder to always exercise caution in interpreting data when there aren't enough observations yet.

Okay, that was the last of the chart types I wanted to cover in more detail. We'll cover pivot charts when we cover pivot tables. They'll use these same chart types, the main difference is basically where the data is coming from.

For now, though, let's talk about all the bells and whistles you can add to a chart and how to edit charts to make them look exactly how you want. (Some of which I've been doing behind the scenes already.)

Charts – Editing and Formatting

If you look back at the screenshots I showed you in the last section you will notice that the charts have descriptive titles that tell you what type of chart it is. And that some of the charts are different sizes or shapes and that they don't use the default color palette.

That's because I edited them. There are a large number of edits you can make to charts.

Let me start with those basic things I did in the last section and then we'll go through more systematically.

Resize a Chart

To resize a chart, click on the chart. You will then see big circles appear at each corner and in the middle of each side of the chart. Like this:

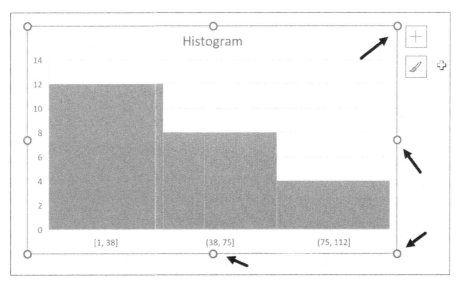

Left-click on one of those circles and drag to change the size of your chart.

To resize both the top and side at once, click and drag from one of the corners. If you do so at an angle, the chart should resize proportionately. All of the elements within the chart space should also resize to fit the new dimensions.

I find resizing charts essential when I include data tables with my charts like I did in one of the examples above. And I usually use this click and drag method because I'm a visual person so I want to resize to what "looks right".

But you can also go to the Format tab that appears for your chart when you click on it and on the far right-hand side you'll see a Size section where you can type in a new value for height, width, or both. Just click into each box and type your new value.

That expansion arrow in the corner of the Size section will open the task pane for Format Chart Area where you can also enter specific values. Clicking on Lock Aspect Ratio will make sure that any change you make to one value (height or width) will also be reflected in the other value (width or height) so that the proportion of width to height remains the same.

Move a Chart

You can also move a chart from where Excel places it. Left-click on the chart and drag to move it to a new location in your workspace. Be careful when you click on the chart that you click somewhere on the chart that doesn't have a chart element, like the title. Because if you click on a chart element you may end up moving the element around instead of the chart.

Charts can also be copied or cut and pasted using the Ctrl shortcuts (Ctrl + C, Ctrl + X, Ctrl + V) or the menu options. This is how I normally move them.

If you right-click and choose Move Chart from the dropdown menu it will show you a dialogue box that will let you move the chart to a different worksheet or a new worksheet. If you choose to move to a new worksheet it will be one that has no cells in it. And you can't undo that move or cut the chart from that worksheet, so the only way to put the chart back in its original location is to right-click and choose to move it again and then select the original worksheet as the location.

The Move Chart option can also be found in the Location section of the Chart Design tab.

When you move a chart to a new worksheet, workbook, or other Office document, your data does not move, only the chart does. (Which is usually what you want, but something to be aware of regardless.) Depending on how you pasted the chart it may still be impacted by any changes to that source data.

Change the Chart Title

To change the title of your chart, click on the name of the chart. Click again on the name to see your cursor blinking amidst the text. Select the text for the current name and then type in what you want to use. (If you want to replace the entire title, Ctrl + A will highlight the current title which will be replaced when you start typing.)

Move Elements Within a Chart

You can move the elements in a chart by clicking on them and then left-clicking and dragging or clicking on a circle in one of the corners to change the shape or size. If an element in a chart can be moved or have its size/shape changed, it will show that frame with circles.

Change A Field Name Used in the Legend

The best bet is to do this in the actual data table that is the source of the data used in the chart. But if that's not possible, use the Select Data option in the Chart Design tab. In the Select Data Source dialogue box, click on the field name, then click on Edit. In the Edit Series or Axis Labels dialogue box that appears, type in the new name in the Series Name or Axis Label Range field.

* * *

Chart Design Tab Options

Okay. Those were the quick basics that I almost always need. Now let's be more systematic about this and walk through the editing options in the Chart Design tab (which can be found to the right of the Help tab when you click on a chart).

Let's start with those options there on the right-hand side, Switch Row/Column, Select Data, and Change Chart Type.

Switch Row/Column

This is the one that makes it irrelevant which data you put across the top or down the side in your data table for a standard bar/column chart or line graph. Because if you find when you create your chart that the wrong variable is along the bottom or the wrong variable is shown in the main chart space, you can flip them using this.

If you use the Insert Chart dialogue box to insert your charts you probably will never even need to do this, because that way of inserting charts shows you both choices:

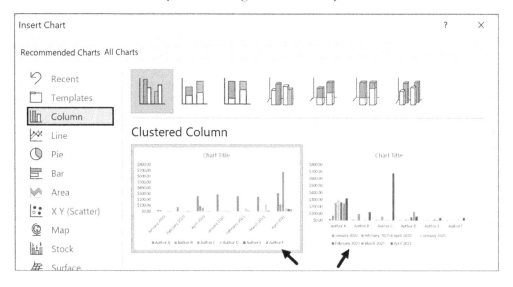

It may be a little hard to see, but the two clustered column choices in the screenshot above have different X axis values. One is showing months on the X axis and then plotting the data by author name for each of those months. The other is showing author names on the X axis and then plotting the data by month for each author name.

Clicking that Switch Row/Column button basically moves you between those two choices.

It's only available when there is data to switch (all of the chart types we discussed except for histograms have it available) and it sometimes won't make any sense to use it (for pie and doughnut charts for example).

Select Data

The Select Data option opens the Select Data Source dialogue box.

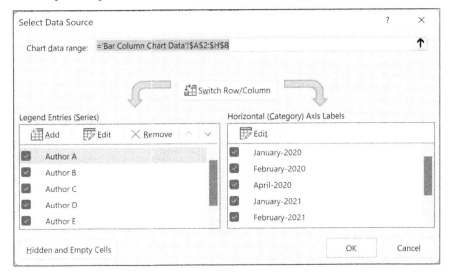

You can do a number of things here.

First, you can switch row/column by clicking on that option in the center of the dialogue box.

Second, you can uncheck the boxes for any of the inputs to the x- or y-axis to exclude them from the chart. This is where I would go to drop Author A, for example, if Author A's data was dominating a chart and I couldn't adequately see the other results.

Third, as mentioned above, you can click on Edit and edit the name for each series of data if you can't edit that name in the data table that's the source for the chart.

And, fourth, you can change the range of the data that's being used by clicking into the Chart Data Range field and changing the cell notation to your new data range.

I prefer to change my data range in the data table itself, however, so let me walk you through how to do that real quick.

First step is to click onto the chart that's using that data table. That will highlight the cells in your data table that are being used by that chart.

Here I have a data table that shows sales for Authors A through F, but if you look at the data table only the data for Authors A through E is highlighted.

	A	B	C	D	E	F	G	H	I
1									
2		January-2020	February-2020	April-2020	May-2020	June-2020	July-2020	August-2020	Total
3	Author A	$23.60	$74.26	$262.40	$296.36	$266.15	$250.00	$322.00	$1,494.77
4	Author B	$17.13	$6.88	$95.68	$3.44	$6.88	$5.59	$121.00	$256.60
5	Author C	$8.44	$6.01	$61.76	$8.98	$5.34	$1.47	$681.81	$773.80
6	Author D	$8.63	$0.52	$13.86	$22.08	$50.85	$128.46	$61.22	$285.62
7	Author E	$3.38	$0.07	$2.74	$3.47	$16.05	$11.24	$42.12	$79.07
8	Author F	$1.69	$0.06	$1.29	$1.33	$3.78	$7.14	$40.8	$56.12
9									

The cells that are being used are shaded differently and there is a colored line around them indicating which part of the chart those cells populate.

To expand the chart to include Author F, I need to left-click and drag in the bottom right corner of either the Author E cell or the last sales entry for Author E (see arrows in image above).

That will bring the selection down to include the row for Author F. Doing either the cell that contains Author E or that last cell with sales data should select the entire next row, including the author name and author sales data for Author F. (If it doesn't, you'll have to do them both separately. I want to say that I have to do that for my line graph of sales, ad spend, and profit, for example.)

When your mouse is appropriately positioned, the cursor should be an angled line with arrows on each end. It's a little hard to see, but here's a screenshot of what that looks like:

	A	B	C	D	E
3	Author A	$23.60	$74.26	$262.40	$296.36
4	Author B	$17.13	$6.88	$95.68	$3.44
5	Author C	$8.44	$6.01	$61.76	$8.98
6	Author D	$8.63	$0.52	$13.86	$22.08
7	Author E	$3.38	$0.07	$2.74	$3.47
8	Author F	$1.69	$0.06	$1.29	$1.33
9					

Once your mouse looks like that, just left-click and drag to select the rest of the data you need. (Note that you can also drag upward if you want to use less data in your chart, but usually I'm adding more data using this method.)

Okay. So to recap: click on the chart, find the edge of the current data range, left-click and drag to make it include my other cells.

But, as mentioned, you can also do so by editing the text in the Select Data dialogue box.

Change Chart Type

To change the chart type for an existing chart, click on the chart, and then click on this option. It brings up the Change Chart dialogue box which is identical to the Insert Chart dialogue box. Click on the new chart type you want and then choose OK.

* * *

Okay, now let's move on to the formatting options on the left-hand side of the Chart Design tab:

Chart Styles

I'm going to continue working right to left because that final option (Add Chart Element) is going to be a doozy.

Chart Styles are pre-formatted styles that you can apply to your chart. They will vary based upon what kind of chart you use. Click on the downpointing arrow in the bottom right corner (noted in the screenshot above) to expand the selections list and see all available options at once, like here where there are fourteen possible column chart styles available:

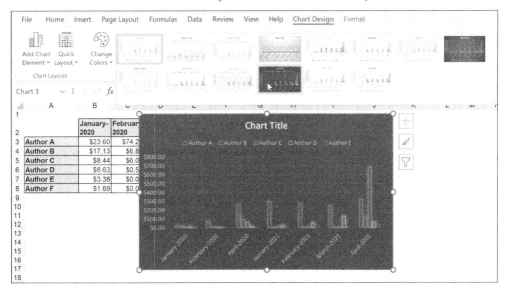

You can also just use the up and down arrows on the right-hand side to see more options (if there are any).

Hold your mouse over each option to see it applied to your chart.

Above I'm looking at one with a black background and different outline and fill color used for each column.

For me personally these styles never are what I want. But they can be a good way to get close to what you want and then tweak from there.

Change Colors

The change colors dropdown allows you to change from Excel's default color scheme, which for me has blue, orange, gray, and yellow for the first four choices, to one of the color schemes shown in the dropdown.

I actually did this for the charts in the last section because I wanted to make sure that a black and white image of that chart in the print books would still have clear differences between the different variables in each chart.

The monochromatic options all work for that. I went with a blue choice so that the ebooks would still have color in them, but I could have chosen monochromatic palettes 3, 7, or 10 if I wanted to only use shades of gray and black.

As with Chart Styles, you can hold your mouse over each choice and see what it will look like before you make your selection by clicking on it.

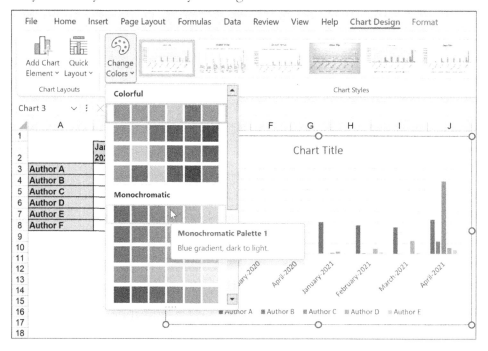

Quick Layout

The quick layout dropdown is another one that shows different potential layouts for your data and will vary based on chart type. It doesn't include different formatting like the Chart Styles do, but is more about including different chart elements.

You can hold your mouse over each one to see it applied and see what it's supposed to include:

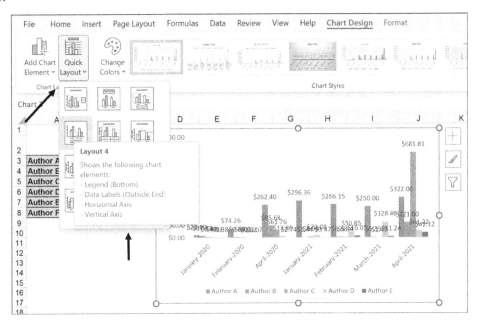

Even when the option is ugly, like this one above, it can give you an idea of which chart elements you may want in your own chart.

Click on the option if you want to keep it.

Be careful if you want to use both Quick Layout and Chart Style because they may overwrite one another. Quick Layout will keep the colors of a Chart Style but may change other elements. Chart Style can sometimes appear to completely replace a Quick Layout, but not always. So the best bet is to see where you end up at the end and use Ctrl + Z if needed to undo.

Or you can get ideas from both of them and then add your own chart elements and formatting, which we'll discuss now, starting with the chart elements.

Add Chart Element

This is where I do most of my chart editing. I almost always want a data table under the chart which means I also remove the chart legend. And I also like to use trendlines sometimes.

To see the list of available Chart Elements, click on the dropdown arrow next to Add Chart Element.

The available options vary by chart type since not all chart types can use all of the chart elements listed. Grayed-out elements are not available for that chart type, like here where Lines and Up/Down Bars are not available options.

Each element will have a secondary dropdown with the choices for that element. Hold your mouse over the element name to see the available options and then hold your mouse over each choice to see it applied temporarily to your chart. Click on the choice to apply it permanently.

Here you can see the choices for Axes, Primary Horizontal and Primary Vertical.

Clicking on the More [X] Options choice at the bottom of the dropdown opens the task pane for formatting that element, which is where the most options are available.

Now let's walk through each option and what it does:

Axes

Axes allows you to add or remove the data point labels on each axis. For example, I sometimes will share a line chart of sales data on my blog but I don't feel the need to share the dollar values involved or sometimes even the months covered by that data, so I remove those labels from my chart.

Here I have removed the $ values from the y-axis and months from the x-axis but the overall trends across periods are still clear.

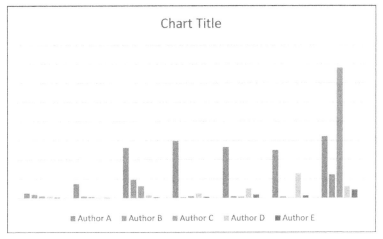

(If this were a chart I was going to share with others I'd need to change the title so others would know what is being plotted here. Something like "Author Revenues Over Time.")

Axis Titles

Axis titles are the text that tells you what each axis contains. You can add or remove them through this menu option.

By default they are not applied. Adding one creates a text box with the text "Axis Title". You then need to edit that text to whatever descriptor you want to use. See below for an example of a chart with an axis title (Months Covered).

Chart Title

The chart title option lets you add, move, or remove a chart title.

There is one present by default that is centered above the chart. You can also place the chart title in a centered overlay position where it's in the center but on the contents of the chart. Like so:

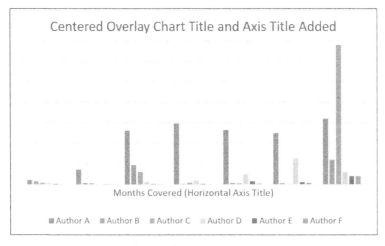

See how the horizontal gridlines run behind the text? With the Above Chart option, they'd all be below the title.

Data Labels

Data labels show the specific value for each data point. They are not present by default.

With most charts you can hold your mouse over any column, bar, data point, pie slice, etc. to see the actual specific value for that data point, even when it's not visible on the chart itself.

But sometimes you want the values showing on the chart. I find this particularly necessary with pie charts which are showing a percentage share because I also want to know the dollar value for that data point.

Here is a pie chart with data labels using the Outside End option:

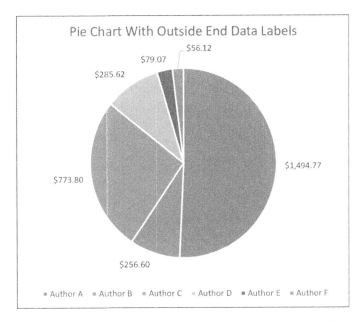

Sometimes two data labels will be too close together and you can't read them because they're on top of each other. That happened in the image above with the $79.07 and $56.12 at the top of the pie chart.

To fix that, click on the data label you want to move and then left-click and drag to move it to a better position. Excel will add a line from the data label to the element it's associated with so you can still see which label belongs to which element in the chart. (You can see that above with the $56.12.)

Data Table

This is one I use often. It places a table below the chart of all of the values that were used to create the chart. I always choose the "with legend keys" choice because that lets me get rid of the legend. If you use that option, the data table can serve both purposes.

When I add one of these, I almost always need to increase the height of the table to show all of the data. Depending on how much data you're including, the data table can at times be bigger than the chart itself.

Also, it's important when using a data table to think about the format of your data in the source data table. I often will format that data in the source table to remove the cents portion of my values so they take up less room.

Error Bars

Error bars lets you add bars to your chart that show standard error, standard deviation, or percentage error in your data. You can also customize the error bars in the task pane to show what a X% error range would be for that data point. If you're curious about how Excel calculates the values, see the Help text for error bars. This is one I recommend you only use if you know what you're doing.

Gridlines

Gridlines are those lines that run behind the chart space that let you more easily track from a data point to its value along an axis. If you want more lines than you're seeing on the chart, you can add minor lines. The default is usually major horizontal lines.

Legend

The legend is what tells you which color in the chart goes with which variable. You can add or remove a legend using this option and you can also choose whether the legend is displayed on the top, bottom, left, or right of the chart.

I definitely recommend having one if you don't have a data table with legends included and there's more than one primary variable shown in the chart. (When in doubt preview it and see if it helps.) Legends are generally included by default in chart types that need them.

Lines

The lines option allows you to add high-low lines or drop lines to a line chart. High-low lines basically connect the highest and lowest value for a time period or observation. Drop lines go from the highest value down to the axis. If you need them you probably know how to use them.

Trendline

A trendline looks at your values and estimates an overall line that shows the direction of those values. This is one I like to use often for things like profit and loss or revenue.

If you have multiple lines in a chart, you have to add one trendline per line. It will by default be a dotted line in the same color as the line it's related to.

Be careful choosing which type of trendline to add. Your choices are linear, exponential, linear forecast, and moving average.

In this chart below I have four trendlines, two each for Authors A and B.

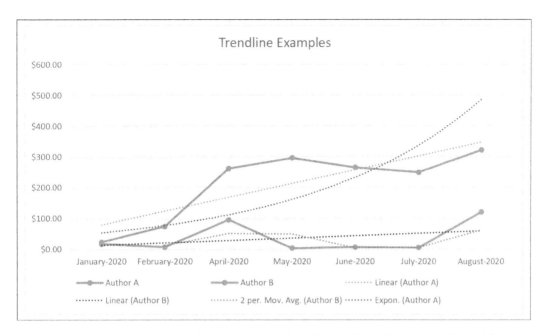

For Author A the straight dotted line that's colored blue is a linear trendline. The curved dotted line that's colored purple is an exponential line.

Of the two, the straight dotted line is the better fit, because Excel doesn't allow a logarithmic trendline choice which is what would likely best fit this data.

For Author B the dark purple dotted line is the linear trendline and the red dotted line that goes up and down is the moving average trendline.

While the linear trendline is close at the beginning and end points, it has no relationship whatsoever to the points in between. This is not linear data. The moving average line doesn't help much either. Although it does better fit the results than the linear line.

Sometimes trendlines help, sometimes they don't. You have to see your data plotted first to decide.

Up/Down Bars

Up/Down Bars connect the first data series data point to the last data series data point.

These get added by default in stock charts.

* * *

Customize Formatting

Okay. So that was a discussion of the various elements you can add or remove from a chart.

Now let's talk about how to customize your formatting. We're going to start with the Format tab that's available when you click on a chart. The formatting options are located in the middle of that Format tab:

Shape Styles are preformatted styles that use different outline colors, interior colors and formats, and text colors (white or black, depending). Click on the downward pointing arrow to see all of the available styles at once. You'll mostly use these for the chart elements like columns or bars, but they can also be applied to text boxes, such as the one around a chart title.

WordArt Styles are for text and involve various text effects such as shadows, beveling, outline colors, fill colors, and patterns. (I don't recommend using them, to be honest.)

In addition, to the right side of both Shape Styles and WordArt Styles are options for fill, outline, and effects that allow you to completely customize the appearance of the shape and text elements in your chart.

To apply these formats to a chart element, you first need to select the element in the chart that you want to format.

So if I want to convert my blue column to a different color, I'd click on one example of that blue column in the chart. That should select all other instances of the blue column. They'll all be outlined and have those circles at the corners like you can see here:

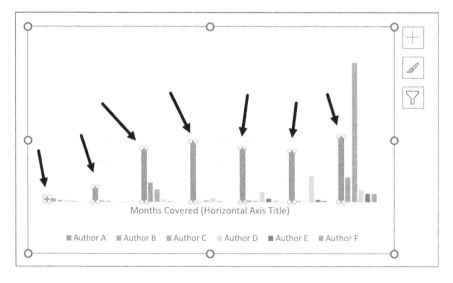

Once all instances of an element are selected, you can then click on the formatting option you want to apply. Holding your mouse over an option will temporarily apply it. Click to permanently apply it.

In this case, if I wanted to apply a different color to that column I could use the Shape Fill dropdown menu to choose a new color.

Or here, for example, I'm holding my mouse over a Shape Style that uses a white fill color with a green outline and you can see it applied to those five columns in the background.

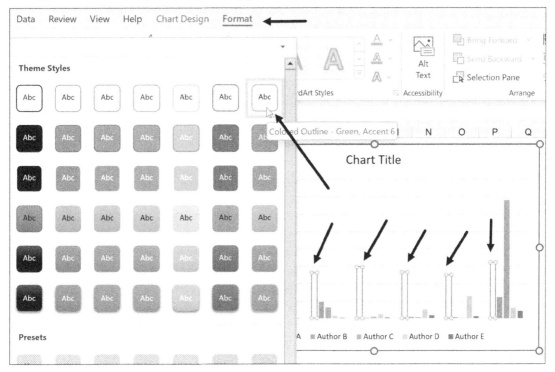

A few more tips on using these options.

With pie and doughnut charts, make sure that you only select one slice or section. It's very easy to select them all at once for some reason, so check which slices are outlined before you apply a format. Usually, I have to click on the slice or section I want to format twice to make sure it's the only one selected.

Use Shape Fill to change the color of columns, bars, pie wedges, etc. Use Shape Outline to change the color of lines.

You can use both shape fill and shape outline on columns, bars, etc. to give a border color around a shape that is different from the interior, like we saw above with the green outline and white fill.

If the fill color is not white, the border may not be obvious. You can adjust the line weight using the Weight option in the Shape Outline dropdown menu. (Unlike with borders, you don't have to adjust the weight first before applying the color. As long as the elements are still selected, you can adjust the line weight at any point in time.)

In addition to color changes and line weight, the dropdowns for fill, outline, and effects allow a number of other formatting choices like adding a gradient or texture, using a picture, adding edges and shadows, etc.

Feel free to explore them. Just be sure if you go down that path that you're not overwhelming the data in the chart with weird formatting. There can be a tendency for newer users to get so excited with all the bells and whistles that Excel offers that they lose the point of what they're doing.

A chart is meant to effectively convey information about complex data in a simple and intuitive manner. If the formatting you add to a chart is not helping do that, don't use it.

That's why I'm not going to go into more detail here on these formatting options, because you can do all sorts of things to your shapes and text in your chart, but you probably shouldn't.

* * *

Chart Task Pane

We've touched on the chart task pane with respect to charts a few times now, but I wanted to address it specifically.

The chart task pane is definitely the most thorough option for formatting a chart. And if you want to, you can start with it when you decide to format.

(I don't use it by default because I don't think it's as intuitive to use as the Format tab.)

To open the task pane, right-click on your chart and choose the Format [X] option towards the bottom of the dropdown menu.

What option is listed will vary depending on where you are on the chart when you right-click. For example, I had various choices like Format Data Series, Format Gridlines, Format Plot Area, Format Chart Area, etc.

Any of those will open the chart task pane on the right-hand side of your worksheet.

The chart task pane is dynamic so the task pane you see will depend on where you were in the chart when you opened it. You can change what you're seeing using the dropdown arrow next to that top options header, which in this case is Chart Options:

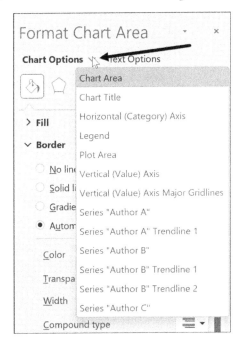

Above, for example, we have the option to change it to edit settings related to the chart area, chart title, horizontal axis, legend, plot area, etc.

Each task pane has icons at the top that you can click on to see various options. Hold your mouse over the icon to see what it covers. Here, for example, the middle icon is for effects:

When you click on one of those icons, the pane will show various categories of settings. So above you can see Shadow, Glow, Soft Edges, and 3-D Format. Click on the arrow to the left of each category to expand it and see the settings for that category like I have above for 3-D Format.

The chart task pane is the only way I know where you can "explode" a pie chart. If you explode a pie chart you take the individual slices and move them outward from the center so that there's more space between them.

To do this, click on the pie chart portion of the pie chart and then right-click and choose Format Data Series to open the task pane. Change the task pane settings until you are in Series Options and have clicked on the third icon which is also Series Options. Pie explosion is the setting at the bottom. Use the slider or change the percentage to "explode" the pie until there's enough space between the slices for what you wanted.

This is a pie chart with a 10% explosion setting:

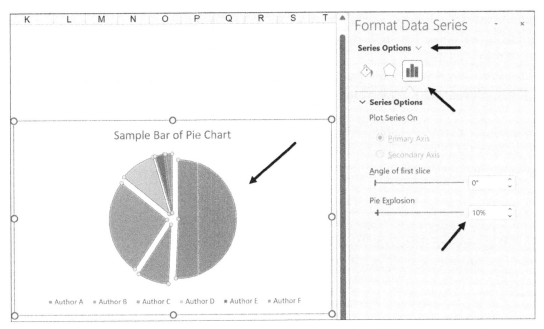

This is also where I go to change the pie chart labels to % values. This can be done in the Label Options section. (Label Options, Label Options, uncheck the box for Value and check the box for Percentage.)

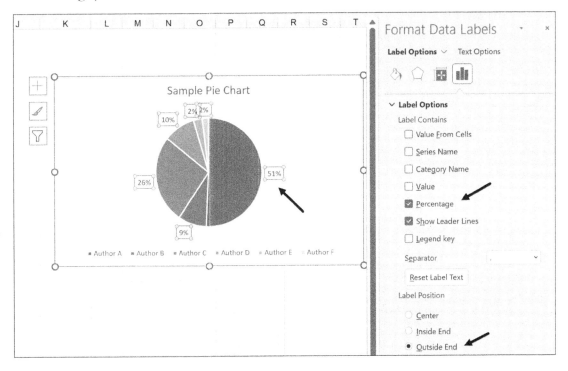

In this case, I did have to add labels using the Chart Design tab first. That could just be my unfamiliarity with the chart task pane, but it seems to only provide options for elements that are already in your chart.

Also, for histograms the chart task pane is the only way I know to customize the bins. As mentioned above, that's under Horizontal Axis, Axis Options, and then the Axis Options section.

Basically, if there's something you want to do with a chart that you think should be possible and you can't find it elsewhere, it's probably somewhere in the chart task pane. (Also, try the Help function which is pretty robust for charts.)

* * *

Alright, that was the basics of charts. Let's take a bit of a breather and cover grouping and subtotaling data and then we can dive in on our next big topic, pivot tables.

Group Data

Okay, let's cover a simpler topic now, grouping data. In *Excel 365 for Beginners* I covered how to hide or unhide columns and rows. (Select them, right-click, choose Hide from the dropdown menu. To unhide, select on either side of the hidden rows or columns, right-click, choose Unhide.)

But that's a more permanent option than what I like to use sometimes. I have worksheets I've created where there are columns that I routinely want next to one another when I'm adding data, but that I don't want next to each other all the time.

Like here with my advertising tracking worksheet:

E	F	G	H	I
Title	ASIN	Author	Series	Advertiser
A19 Beginner	B08Y852VDZ	M.L. Humphrey	Access Essentials 2019	Amazon CPC
Office 2019 Beginner	B095Q278NW	M.L. Humphrey	Office Essentials	Amazon CPC
Apub for Ads	B09RNBB9JF	M.L. Humphrey	Affinity Publisher	Amazon CPC
E19 Charts	B08WN7RMBQ	M.L. Humphrey	Easy Excel Essentials 201	Amazon CPC
Mail Merge for Beginners	B07QQ2T6GX	M.L. Humphrey	Mail Merge Essentials	Amazon CPC
Tables	B07QNZWJTP	M.L. Humphrey	Easy Word Essentials	Amazon CPC
Charts	B07DGHM1LM	M.L. Humphrey	Easy Excel Essentials	Amazon CPC

Column E is the title of the book I was advertising. Columns F, G, and H are information I want about that book, but not information I have to input myself. (I used VLOOKUP to populate those columns.) Column I is who I advertised with.

You can't see it, but Column J is how much I spent and then there are click and performance measurements after that.

When I'm inputting my advertising data, I don't want to see Columns F, G, and H. But at other times I do want them visible. So I need a solution that lets me toggle back and forth between having them hidden and not hidden. That's what grouping does. I can group my columns and then I just have to click on the minus sign for that group to hide those columns or the plus sign to see them.

Let's walk through how to do this now. I have moved a sample of that data into a new worksheet with Title in Column A, ASIN, Author, and Series in Columns B, C, and D, and then Advertiser in Column E.

To be able to group Columns B, C, and D, I have to select them first. (So click on the letter for Column B or for Column D and then left-click and drag to select all three.) Next, I go to the Outline section at the end of the Data tab and click on Group.

When you group a set of rows or columns you will see a gray area above the columns or to the left of the rows which will initially have a line with a minus sign at the end that spans the grouped columns or rows. Like this:

When the grouped columns or rows are visible you'll see that minus sign at the end. Click on it to collapse the group and hide the columns or rows.

When you do that you'll see a plus sign in that gray area above where the columns were and they'll be hidden. Note how this goes from Column A to Column E:

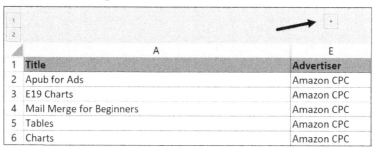

Simply click on that plus sign to show those columns or rows once more. (There are also options in the Outline section of the Data tab to Show Detail or Hide Detail, which are to the right of Group and Ungroup, but by default it shouldn't be necessary to use them, because you have the plus and minus signs to use. If you ever get rid of those, though, that is another way to show or hide your grouped columns or rows.)

To remove grouping from a worksheet, go back to the Outline section of the Data tab and choose Clear Outline from the Ungroup dropdown menu. This will remove all groups in that worksheet as long as you didn't have one specific group selected.

If you select only one set of grouped columns or rows, Clear Outline will just remove that grouping.

Ungroup also works to remove grouping. You have to select all cells in the worksheet or those grouped rows or columns first, then click on Ungroup, and then when the dialogue box appears choose either rows or columns, and then click OK.

You cannot undo Ungrouping. Ctrl + Z does not work to reverse that, so if you accidentally ungroup your worksheet and didn't mean to, you'll need to build it back manually.

One final note, you can only group columns or rows that are next to one another. So if you can't select them using left-click and drag or the Shift key, Excel won't let you group them. You'll get an error message when you try to.

Subtotal Data

In that same Outline section of the Data tab there is also an option to Subtotal, which takes a data table and performs a calculation each time there is a change in the value in the designated column. So, a sum of revenue for each change in customer name, for example.

The first step when subtotaling your data is to sort it properly. If you want to subtotal by each change in X column, then you need to sort X column so that all like values are grouped together. (I'll show you in a minute what happens if you don't do that.)

The next step is to select your data, go to the Outline section of the Data tab, and click on Subtotal.

This will bring up the Subtotal dialogue box. Here you can see the data we're going to use for this sample as well as the dialogue box:

The dialogue box will be pre-populated with default suggestions, but you can change them.

The first choice is what column is driving your subtotals. In this case I'm going to change that to Title. The data is split between two titles, Title A and Title B.

The next choice is what calculation you want Excel to perform. The default is to sum the values in a column, but you can also choose to count the values, average them, return the minimum value, return the maximum value, calculate the product of the values, count the numbers, or calculate different types of variance or standard deviation.

I'm going to leave that as sum.

The next choice is which columns you want to perform those calculations for. You only get that one choice, sum, average, etc. but you can perform it for multiple columns. Just check the boxes for each one you want.

I'm going to do Units Sold, Units Refunded, and Net Units Sold.

Check "replace current subtotals" when you're editing a data table that already has them.

If you want the results to print out on separate pages for each change in the variable, check the box for "page break between groups". And if you want a grand total value as well, make sure the box for "summary below data" is checked.

By default it will replace any existing subtotals and provide a summary. I chose to also have the page break between groups just to show you how that appears in your workspace. Here we go:

	Royalty Date	Title	Author Name	Marketplace	Royalty Type	Transaction Type	Units Sold	Units Refunded	Net Units Sold
1	Royalty Date	Title	Author Name	Marketplace	Royalty Type	Transaction Type	Units Sold	Units Refunded	Net Units Sold
2	2021-01-31	Book Title A	Author A	Amazon.com	70%	Standard	1	0	1
3	2021-01-31	Book Title A	Author B	Amazon.com.au	70%	Standard	1	0	1
4	2021-01-31	Book Title A	Author C	Amazon.com	70%	Free - Price Match	65	0	65
5	2021-01-31	Book Title A	Author D	Amazon.com	70%	Standard	1	0	1
6	2021-01-31	Book Title A	Author C	Amazon.fr	70%	Free - Price Match	1	0	1
7	2021-01-31	Book Title A	Author C	Amazon.ca	70%	Free - Price Match	3	0	3
8	2021-01-31	Book Title A	Author A	Amazon.com	70%	Standard	1	0	1
9	2021-01-31	Book Title A	Author C	Amazon.de	70%	Free - Price Match	3	0	3
10	2021-01-31	Book Title A	Author A	Amazon.com	35%	Standard	1	0	1
11	2021-01-31	Book Title A	Author A	Amazon.com	70%	Standard	1	0	1
12	2021-01-31	Book Title A	Author A	Amazon.com	70%	Standard	1	0	1
13	2021-01-31	Book Title A	Author D	Amazon.com	70%	Standard	2	0	2
14		Book Title A Total					81	0	81
15	2021-01-31	Book Title B	Author D	Amazon.com	70%	Standard	1	0	1
16	2021-01-31	Book Title B	Author F	Amazon.com	35%	Free - Price Match	1	0	1
17	2021-01-31	Book Title B	Author A	Amazon.co.uk	70%	Standard	1	0	1
18	2021-01-31	Book Title B	Author A	Amazon.com	35%	Standard	1	0	1
19	2021-01-31	Book Title B	Author C	Amazon.com	35%	Free - Price Match	5	0	5
20	2021-01-31	Book Title B	Author D	Amazon.com	70%	Standard	1	0	1
21	2021-01-31	Book Title B	Author C	Amazon.com	70%	Standard	2	0	2
22	2021-01-31	Book Title B	Author A	Amazon.com	70%	Standard	1	0	1
23	2021-01-31	Book Title B	Author A	Amazon.com	70%	Standard	1	0	1
24	2021-01-31	Book Title B	Author A	Amazon.com	70%	Standard	1	0	1
25	2021-01-31	Book Title B	Author A	Amazon.com	70%	Standard	1	0	1
26	2021-01-30	Book Title B	Author B	Amazon.com.au	70%	Standard	1	0	1
27	2021-01-30	Book Title B	Author C	Amazon.com	70%	Free - Price Match	8	0	8
28		Book Title B Total					25	0	25
29		Grand Total					106	0	106
30									

Look at Row 14 where there is a subtotal for Book Title A. And then Row 28 is the subtotal for Book Title B. And Row 29 is the total for both. On the left-hand side are grouping lines that let you collapse either the details for Book Title A or the details for Book Title B (under group 2) or that let you collapse everything and just show the grand total row (under group 1).

That line you can see under Row 14 is the page break, but you'd have to go to print preview to actually see the data separated out onto a separate page.

As you can see, subtotal also groups data. But you can remove the grouping by using the Clear Outline option under Ungroup. That will leave the subtotals but remove the grouping and ability to collapse the various levels of the data table.

To remove subtotals, go back to Subtotal and when the Subtotal dialogue box opens, click on the Remove All button at the bottom left corner of the dialogue box.

Now let me show you what happens if you don't sort your data first. I'm going to do exactly the same thing, but for Author Name. There are five author names in this data. Let's see if we get five groups:

	Royalty Date	Title	Author Name	Marketplace	Royalty Type	Transaction Type	Units Sold	Units Refunded	Net Units Sold
1	Royalty Date	Title	Author Name	Marketplace	Royalty Type	Transaction Type	Units Sold	Units Refunded	Net Units Sold
3			Author A Total				1	0	1
5			Author B Total				1	0	1
7			Author C Total				65	0	65
9			Author D Total				1	0	1
12			Author C Total				4	0	4
14			Author A Total				1	0	1
16			Author C Total				3	0	3
20			Author A Total				3	0	3
23			Author D Total				3	0	3
25			Author F Total				1	0	1
28			Author A Total				2	0	2
30			Author C Total				5	0	5
32			Author D Total				1	0	1
34			Author C Total				2	0	2
39			Author A Total				4	0	4
41			Author B Total				1	0	1
43			Author C Total				8	0	8
44									
45									
46									
47			Grand Total				106	0	106

No.

I clicked on the 2 on the left-hand side to collapse everything one level and hide each row of detail so that we were only seeing the subtotal rows. As you can see, there are far more than five groups.

If you look closer you'll see that most of the authors have more than one subtotal. Author A, for example, has five subtotals as noted in the image above.

That's because the data was not sorted. And Excel doesn't know better. What it's doing is going down that column and every time the value changes, it subtotals. So when the data changed from Author A to Author B, subtotal. From Author B to Author C, subtotal. And so on and so on down the list. If there were two rows for an author that were next to each other those were grouped and subtotaled together, but otherwise, no.

What else to tell you?

I mentioned that I clicked on the 2 to collapse everything to hide the detail. To bring it back for all rows, I can click on the 3. You can also click on individual plus or minus signs to expand or collapse a particular subset of entries.

Click on the 1 to just show the grand total row.

I had an issue just now where clicking on the 1 hid everything, even the grand total row. I believe this was caused by including blank rows from below the data table when I subtotaled. (I just used Ctrl + A to select all cells in the worksheet.) Going back and more carefully choosing only rows with data in them fixed the issue.

(Don't be afraid to make mistakes in Excel. If you think something should work, go back and try again. Sometimes little quirky things like that will mess you up but what you want to do will in fact be possible.)

If you ever have data that has more grouping levels than that, just think of the 1 as the highest level of grouping and the others as more granular levels of grouping. Let the gray lines in the grouping section guide you. For example, here you can see that Rows 36 and 37 are grouped and will disappear if I click on that minus sign there.

	A	B	C	D	E	F
33	2021-01-31	Book Title B	Author C	Amazon.com		70% Standard
34			**Author C Total**			
35	2021-01-31	Book Title B	Author A	Amazon.com		70% Standard
36	2021-01-31	Book Title B	Author A	Amazon.com		70% Standard
37	2021-01-31	Book Title B	Author A	Amazon.com		70% Standard
38	2021-01-31	Book Title B	Author A	Amazon.com		70% Standard
39			**Author A Total**			
40	2021-01-30	Book Title B	Author B	Amazon.com.au		70% Standard
41			**Author B Total**			
42	2021-01-30	Book Title B	Author C	Amazon.com		70% Free - Price Match
43			**Author C Total**			
44			**Grand Total**			

One final note about subtotals. If you select only the data but not the header row, Excel will show an error message dialogue box and ask if you want to include that header row in your selection. Click on Yes to proceed with that row included. Click on No if you don't want to. If you click on No it will treat the first row of values you did select as a header row. Cancel or closing the dialogue box will take you back to the worksheet without subtotaling.

Pivot Tables – Insert and Build

Introduction

First off, Excel writes pivot table as PivotTable, but I don't like that so I'm not going to do it. I did for the Excel 2019 books, but for this one I've decided not to. They let you search for pivot tables in the help screen just fine, so that's what we're going with.

Pivot tables are fantastic. I learned about them when I was in college and provided support to an Econ researcher who needed me to summarize some data. (He looked at me with horror when I confessed I didn't know what they were, but in my defense this was back in the day when I didn't even have a personal computer and the internet was not a place where I learned things.)

Once I learned about them, I was convinced that they are one of the most valuable tools in Excel. There is no better way to take a table of data and quickly summarize it.

In the beginner book and here I've occasionally used an anonymized version of one of my sales reports from Amazon. The one I'm using has 631 rows that include information for seven different author names with sales in ten different Amazon stores and three different sales types.

I could use filtering to see results for a single author, store, or transaction type. Or even combinations of those three. Or I could sort and then subtotal by one category. But pivot tables are just better. Let me show you.

Insert

Here are the first few rows of the data we're working with:

	A	B	C	D	E	F	G
1	Royalty Date	Author Name	Marketplace	Transaction Ty	Net Units So	Royalty	Currency
2	2021-01-31	Author A	Amazon.com	Standard	1	5.70	USD
3	2021-01-31	Author B	Amazon.com.au	Standard	1	5.03	AUD
4	2021-01-31	Author C	Amazon.com	Free - Price Match	65	0.00	USD
5	2021-01-31	Author D	Amazon.com	Standard	1	2.76	USD
6	2021-01-31	Author C	Amazon.fr	Free - Price Match	1	0.00	EUR
7	2021-01-31	Author A	Amazon.ca	Free - Price Match	3	0.00	CAD
8	2021-01-31	Author A	Amazon.com	Standard	1	5.83	USD
9	2021-01-31	Author C	Amazon.de	Free - Price Match	3	0.00	EUR

Because my worksheet is set up with the header information in the first row and then only rows of data after that, I can just select the whole worksheet. (Ctrl + A or click in the top left corner where that dark gray triangle is.)

You can work with data that starts elsewhere in your document, but what you do need to have is data that has a clear header row, no subtotals or grand totals, and ideally no breaks in columns or rows within the data. Also, no merged cells.

So get your data formatted properly and select it.

Next step is to go to the Insert tab and click on the image for PivotTable in the Tables section. Be sure to click on the image and not the dropdown arrow.

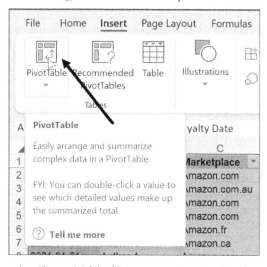

(The image is the same as the From Table/Range option in the dropdown, so if you click on the dropdown arrow accidentally (like I often do) you can just select that option.)

Your other choice there is to use an external data source, something we are not going to cover here. Working with external data increases the risk of something breaking along the way.

The PivotTable From Table Or Range dialogue box will appear.

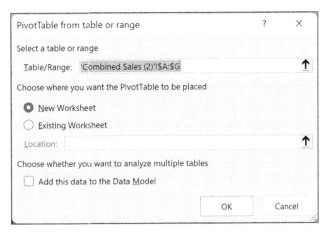

It will show your selected data and then give you the option of putting the table in a new worksheet or an existing worksheet.

I generally do not recommend putting a pivot table in the same worksheet as any other data so I almost always go with new worksheet.

I will on occasion put the pivot table in the same worksheet as my data when I know it's a one-off and that all of my data is already in place.

The reason not to put a pivot table in a worksheet with other data is because pivot tables are dynamic. They will change size and shape based upon what data is feeding into them.

So if I, for example, create a pivot table with author names in it and then add my own analysis text below that or to the right side, and later decide to add marketplace to the pivot table, I will have a problem. Because the pivot table will need to expand to include that new information but won't be able to because of my text. (Excel does at least tell you this is an issue before overwriting the text and gives you the chance to cancel doing so, but it's best to never have to worry about it in the first place.)

If you really do want that pivot table in your same worksheet as your data, then be sure to put it to the right or below any of your other data in that worksheet to avoid problems. Whatever cell you choose for placing the pivot table, Excel will build from that spot over and down.

Okay. So I'm leaving those settings alone because I already selected my data and want to put the table in a new worksheet, which means I can just click OK.

Excel will then open a new worksheet that has a blank pivot table in the main workspace and a PivotTable Fields task pane on the right-hand side.

There are also PivotTable Analyze and Design tabs visible at the top of the workspace which we will cover in detail later. They will only be visible when you are working with the pivot table. Click on it to see them if you click away.

Build

You have two options for building your pivot table. You can check the boxes for the fields you want to include in your pivot table in the top of the task pane and let Excel place the fields for you where it thinks they make the most sense.

Or, and this is the method I use, you can place the fields yourself at the bottom of the task pane by left-clicking on each field name in the top section and dragging it down to one of the Filters, Columns, Rows, or Values boxes.

Here, for example, I have dragged Author Name into the Rows box and Net Units Sold into the Values box:

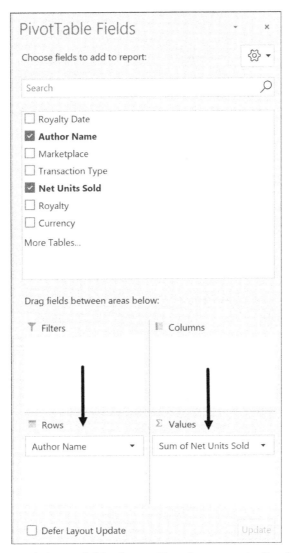

When I clicked and dragged those fields down, Excel automatically checked the box next to each field name in the top section.

That gives me a pivot table that has all of my author names listed on the left-hand side in rows and then, because I don't have anything in the Columns box, it leaves me with one single column next to that where the total number of units for each author is shown. Like so:

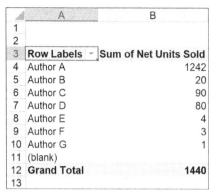

(Excel will automatically decide the type of calculation to perform on any field you put in the Values box. In this case, sum. But if you want to change that you can. We'll discuss how to do so later.)

So there we go. Less than a minute to summarize 600+ rows of data. And I can see all of it in one glance without having to filter or sort or add formulas.

That was the most basic of pivot tables. Now, let's start making more complex pivot tables.

I want to look at amount earned per author, but the problem is that this report includes different currencies, so I can't just sum up the Royalty column for each author because while maybe Euros and Dollars are about the same right now, something like Japanese Yen will throw everything out the window.

What I need is to list the amount earned in each currency for each author.

To do this, I can add Currency to my Columns box and put Royalty into the Values section.

This is what I now have in the pivot table task pane:

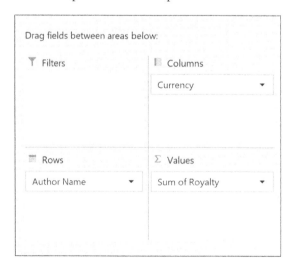

And this is what that pivot table looks like:

	A	B	C	D	E	F	G	H	I	J	K
1											
2											
3	Sum of Royalty	Column Labels									
4	Row Labels	AUD		CAD	EUR	GBP	INR	MXN	USD	(blank)	Grand Total
5	Author A		12.35	108.12	13.03	337.01		40.25	5839.71		6350.47
6	Author B		15.09			28.42			22.79		66.3
7	Author C			0	0	0	0		8.98		8.98
8	Author D		3.79			7.43			293.38		304.6
9	Author E				2.56				14.71		17.27
10	Author F								0		0
11	Author G					0.35					0.35
12	(blank)										
13	Grand Total		31.23	108.12	15.59	373.21	0	40.25	6179.57		6747.97
14											

(We'll cover formatting later.)

Now let's build a pivot table that uses the Filter section to filter the entire pivot table based upon a field value. Here I've created a pivot table that has Author Name in Rows, Net Units Sold and Royalty in Values, and Transaction Type and Marketplace in Filters.

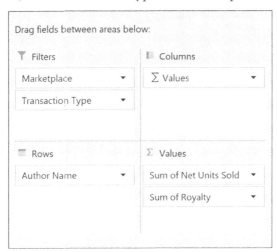

This is how that looks by default:

	A	B	C
1	Marketplace (All)		
2	Transaction Type (All)		
3			
4	Row Labels	Sum of Net Units Sold	Sum of Royalty
5	Author A	1242	6350.47
6	Author B	20	66.3
7	Author C	90	8.98
8	Author D	80	304.6
9	Author E	4	17.27
10	Author F	3	0
11	Author G	1	0.35
12	(blank)		
13	Grand Total	1440	6747.97
14			

But we put in filters for a reason, so let's go to the Transaction Type filter and click on the dropdown arrow:

I want to remove Free – Price Match from that list. To do so, I click on Select Multiple Items down there at the bottom of the dropdown. That's going to put checked boxes by each of the values up top and I can then uncheck Free – Price Match.

(If there are a lot of choices and you only want one, click the checkbox next to Select Multiple Items, and then click the box next to All to unselect all. You can then check the one or two you want. It's easier than unchecking each one individually.)

After you remove some of the values, that All in parens next to the field name will change to either Multiple Items or the one value you've chosen if you chose just one.

Here is that table with Marketplace limited to just one value, Amazon.com, and Transaction Type limited to all but Free — Price Match:

	A	B	C
1	Marketplace	Amazon.com	
2	Transaction Type	(Multiple Items)	
3			
4	**Row Labels**	**Sum of Net Units Sold**	**Sum of Royalty**
5	Author A	1129	5839.71
6	Author B	6	22.79
7	Author C	3	8.98
8	Author D	76	293.38
9	Author E	3	14.71
10	**Grand Total**	**1217**	**6179.57**
11			

To see which fields that Multiple Items is showing (or not showing), you can click on the filter symbol:

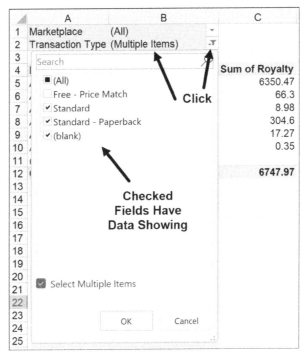

Now let's create an even more-complex pivot table that uses multiple fields for both Rows and Columns.

To do this, I went back to my original data table that's feeding this pivot table and added columns with month and year data and then refreshed the pivot table. (We'll cover Refresh later.)

For this new pivot table, I placed both year and month in Columns, both Author Name and Currency in Rows, and Royalty in Values:

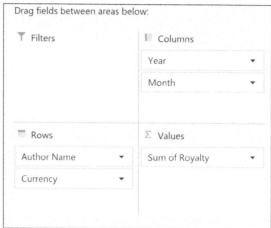

When you have more than one field in Columns or Rows, order matters. In this case I wanted Year to be the highest-level with months below that and then Author to be the highest level with currency below that.

Here's what that looks like:

Row Labels	January	February	March	April	2021 Total	(blank)	(blank) Total	January	February	April	2020 Total	Grand Total
Author A	**350.56**	**342.83**	**3174.69**	**2091.06**	**5959.14**			**28.45**	**96.21**	**266.67**	**391.33**	**6350.47**
AUD	9.96				9.96				2.39		2.39	12.35
CAD	27.14	5.75	47.49	23.85	104.23				3.89		3.89	108.12
EUR	1.66		4.2		5.86				7.17		7.17	13.03
GBP	15.44	30.68	188.53	84.74	319.39			4.85	8.5	4.27	17.62	337.01
MXN			40.25		40.25							40.25
USD	296.36	266.15	2934.47	1982.47	5479.45			23.6	74.26	262.4	360.26	5839.71
Author B	**40.61**	**9.64**	**9.17**		**59.42**				**6.88**		**6.88**	**66.3**
AUD	15.09				15.09							15.09
GBP	22.08	2.76	3.58		28.42							28.42
USD	3.44	6.88	5.59		15.91				6.88		6.88	22.79
Author C	**8.98**				**8.98**			**0**			**0**	**8.98**
CAD	0				0							0
EUR	0				0			0			0	0
GBP	0				0							0
INR	0				0							0
USD	8.98				8.98							8.98
Author D	**22.43**	**54.64**	**128.46**	**68.3**	**273.83**			**8.63**	**8.28**	**13.86**	**30.77**	**304.6**
AUD		3.79			3.79							3.79
GBP	0.35			7.08	7.43							7.43
USD	22.08	50.85	128.46	61.22	262.61			8.63	8.28	13.86	30.77	293.38
Author E	**6.03**		**11.24**		**17.27**							**17.27**
EUR	2.56				2.56							2.56
USD	3.47		11.24		14.71							14.71
Author F	**0**				**0**							**0**
USD	0				0							0
Author G	**0.35**				**0.35**							**0.35**
GBP	0.35				0.35							0.35
(blank)												
(blank)												
Grand Total	**428.96**	**407.11**	**3323.56**	**2159.36**	**6318.99**			**37.08**	**111.37**	**280.53**	**428.98**	**6747.97**

See that each author is listed first with their transactions broken down by currency and that each year of sales is listed first with the transactions by month listed under that.

It looks very complex but what it's showing is how much was earned each month of each year in each currency for each author.

By placing Author above Currency in the Rows section, the data is ordered with each currency listed for each author. If I had instead placed Currency first, it would be listed with each author for each currency. Like this:

	A	B	C	D	E	F
4	Sum of Royalty	Column Labels				
5		2021				2021 Total
6	Row Labels	January	February	March	April	
7	AUD	25.05	3.79			28.84
8	Author A	9.96				9.96
9	Author B	15.09				15.09
10	Author D		3.79			3.79
11	CAD	27.14	5.75	47.49	23.85	104.23
12	Author A	27.14	5.75	47.49	23.85	104.23
13	Author C	0				0
14	EUR	4.22		4.2		8.42
15	Author A	1.66		4.2		5.86
16	Author C	0				0
17	Author E	2.56				2.56
18	GBP	38.22	33.44	192.11	91.82	355.59

See how now the data shows for each currency and then any author who had sales in that currency is listed below that?

Same thing happens in the Rows section.

I put year first and then month so that you have all monthly values listed under each year. If I'd reversed that order you'd have all yearly values listed under each month. So the table would start with January and then show both 2020 and 2021 values for January before then doing the same for February and then March.

Okay. So that's how to build pivot tables. Basically, make sure your data is formatted well for use with a pivot table, select it, insert a pivot table, and then click and drag the fields you want to use into place.

If you have more than one field in Rows or Columns, the order matters. The one listed first is the primary category.

You can put more than one field into the Values section, too, but I don't recommend doing so if the Columns and Rows sections are complex. Basically, step back when you're done and ask yourself if there's so much information in the table that it's too hard to follow. If there is, simplify and maybe use more than one pivot table. Or make some of those fields into filters. (Or add Slicers, which we'll discuss soon.)

Okay. That was the basics of how to insert and build pivot tables, but there's a lot more to this topic. Let's now cover some common tricks for working with a pivot table. Things I did in this chapter that I didn't want to stop to discuss at the time.

Pivot Tables – Work With

In the last chapter there were a number of basic tasks related to pivot tables that I performed but didn't cover or that I wanted to explain. They come up often enough that I wanted to highlight them in their own chapter. But later we'll more systematically go through the pivot table tabs and other options you have related to pivot tables to cover more obscure tasks, too.

So.

Change Calculation Type

We were very lucky in the last chapter that Excel recognized the value for Net Units Sold as a number that it could sum. Often with my data sets I receive from my vendors I am not that lucky. Excel brings in the numeric values in those workbooks as text and then defaults to *counting* the values instead of summing them up.

To fix this, click on the arrow on the right-hand side of the entry in the Values section, and choose Value Field Settings from the dropdown menu. Like here:

This will open the Value Field Settings dialogue box:

If you just want a basic calculation like sum or count it's available right there on the Summarize Values By tab.

You can make different choices for different columns of data if you have more than one field in the Values section. But be careful. Because it may not be immediately obvious that one column is a count, one is a sum of values, and one is an average.

I generally, unless my data labels and formats and other attributes make it abundantly clear, do not mix and match what I'm doing with multiple columns of data. Everything sums. Or everything takes the maximum value. Or everything takes the minimum value. Etc.

But it's a free world, you can do what you want. Just keep your audience in mind and make sure they'll quickly see what you've done.

There are two other ways to open the Value Field Settings dialogue box.

One is to click on an entry in your pivot table and go to the Active Field section of the PivotTable Analyze tab where you will see that field you selected listed. Click on Field Settings to open the Value Field Settings dialogue box and edit the settings for that field.

The other is to right-click on a value in the pivot table and then choose Value Field Settings from the bottom section of that dropdown menu.

All of those options rely on using the Value Field Settings dialogue box. This is my general approach because at the same time I can format the cells.

But, that dropdown also lets you directly choose how to summarize values (sum, count, average, etc.) using the Summarize Values By option, which lists all of those choices in a dropdown menu format.

Use a Comparison Calculation

You can also do a comparison-style calculation with a field in your pivot table instead using the Show Values As tab in the Value Field Settings dialogue box or using the Show Values As dropdown menu:

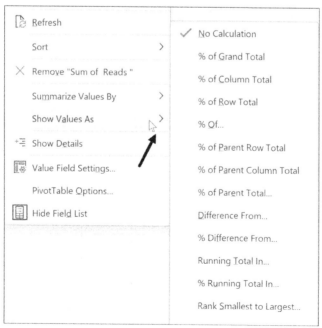

As you can see, there are a large number of choices, such as % of Grand Total, % of Column Total, % of Row Total, and many many more.

You can actually add a field a second time and have one use of the field for a calculation like sum and the other use of the field for a comparison value like % of column total. I've done that here for Net Units Sold:

	A	B	C
1			
2			
3	Row Labels	Sum of Net Units Sold	Sum of Net Units Sold2
4	Author A	1242	86.25%
5	Author B	20	1.39%
6	Author C	90	6.25%
7	Author D	80	5.56%
8	Author E	4	0.28%
9	Author F	3	0.21%
10	Author G	1	0.07%
11	(blank)		0.00%
12	Grand Total	1440	100.00%

We can see that Author A is 86% of the units sold for the data set. Same as taking 1242, the actual total of the net units sold for Author A, and dividing by 1440, the total net units sold for all authors.

I can show both here and it looks fine because we're only looking at one variable, net units sold. If I were to add a second variable, like royalty, that would make things a bit messy, so I'd probably want to choose one or the other, but not display both. Again, think of your audience when building any pivot table or chart. Will they understand what they're seeing?

Remove a Field From a Pivot Table

The easiest way to remove a field from a pivot table is to just uncheck the checkbox in the top of the task pane. But if you used a field more than once like I did above and you want to remove only one of the uses, that won't work.

Another option is to click on the arrow to the right of the field name, and then click Remove Field from the dropdown.

Or you can right-click on one of the values for that field in the actual pivot table and choose the "Remove [X]" option from the dropdown menu, where X is the field name.

You can also left-click and drag the field away from the bottom of the task pane.

Sort Pivot Table Data

One of the things I often like to do when dealing with pivot tables is sort my data. I usually want my most successful authors or titles or series shown at the top of the table.

To sort a pivot table, right-click in a cell in the column where you want to sort, find Sort in the dropdown menu, and then choose the type of sort you want:

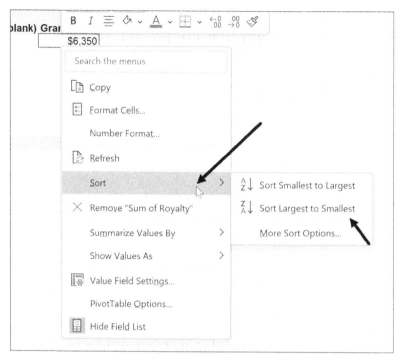

That will sort your data by the values in that selected column, in this case Column J, Grand Total:

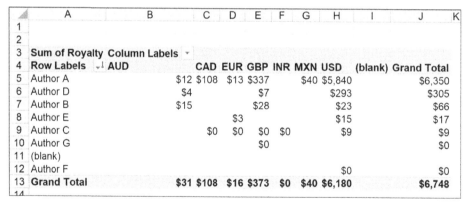

	A	B	C	D	E	F	G	H	I	J	K
1											
2											
3	Sum of Royalty	Column Labels									
4	Row Labels	AUD	CAD	EUR	GBP	INR	MXN	USD	(blank)	Grand Total	
5	Author A		$12	$108	$13	$337		$40	$5,840		$6,350
6	Author D		$4			$7			$293		$305
7	Author B		$15			$28			$23		$66
8	Author E				$3				$15		$17
9	Author C			$0	$0	$0	$0		$9		$9
10	Author G					$0					$0
11	(blank)										
12	Author F								$0		$0
13	Grand Total		$31	$108	$16	$373	$0	$40	$6,180		$6,748
14											

Now I have my largest values at the top and my smallest at the bottom.

Hide Entries in A Pivot Table

You can also hide certain entries by clicking on the arrow next to Row Labels or Column Labels and then unchecking the ones you don't want to see:

It works just like selecting or unselecting values when filtering data. I sometimes have "blank" as values in my tables and I don't need it there so I'll do this to remove it.

Here I made it so that only CAD transactions show:

	A	B	C
1			
2			
3	Sum of Royalty	Column Labels ▾	
4	Row Labels ▾	CAD	Grand Total
5	Author A	$108	$108
6	Author C	$0	$0
7	Grand Total	$108	$108
8			

Note that the arrow turned into a filter so you know that this is not a complete listing of all of your data.

Also, note how the pivot table size changed when I did that. There were only two authors with sales in Canada for that month, so not only did the number of columns go down, but so did the number of rows. Remember, pivot tables are dynamic, they adjust to display data based on your choices as to what to include or not include.

If there are two fields for columns or rows, click on a value in the pivot table for the one you want to edit first so that that's the dropdown menu that you see.

Group Values In a Row or Column in a Pivot Table

You can also group values in a row or column in a pivot table. Values you want to group *do not* have to be located next to each other. Select the values you want to group by clicking on the first one and then using Ctrl or Shift or clicking and dragging to select more.

Below I've chosen Authors C, E, and G, for example, by holding down Ctrl as I clicked on each one.

Once the values you want to group have been selected, right-click and choose Group from the dropdown menu:

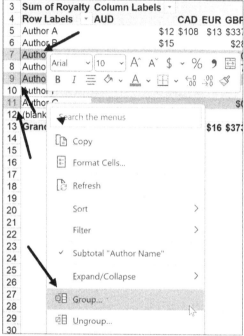

That will create a new level in that table for groups where the grouped values you selected are in one group and all other values are in their own group that only contains them and is named after them. Like so:

Sum of Royalty	Column Labels								
Row Labels	AUD	CAD	EUR	GBP	INR	MXN	USD	(blank)	Grand Total
Author A		$12	$108	$13	$337		$40	$5,840	$6,350
Author A		$12	$108	$13	$337		$40	$5,840	$6,350
Author B	$15			$28			$23		$66
Author B	$15			$28			$23		$66
Group1		$0	$3	$0	$0		$24		$27
Author C		$0	$0	$0	$0		$9		$9
Author E			$3				$15		$17
Author G				$0					$0
Author D	$4			$7			$293		$305
Author D	$4			$7			$293		$305
Author F							$0		$0
Author F							$0		$0
(blank)									
(blank)									
Grand Total	$31	$108	$16	$373	$0	$40	$6,180		$6,748

Group 1 contains Authors C, E, and G and then all of the other authors (and blank) have their own group.

The PivotTable Analyze tab also has a Group section where you can either group entries or ungroup them. You'll need to select your items first before you can use it.

Rename Group

When you click on a group name you should also see that name in your formula bar. You can edit the name by going to the formula bar and typing in what you want to use for that group:

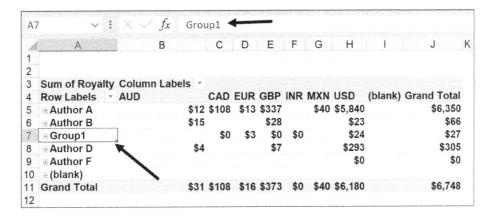

Collapse Groups

You can collapse the groups, like I have in the screenshot above, by right-clicking on a group name, going to Expand/Collapse in the dropdown menu, and choosing Collapse Entire Field.

6	Autho	Search the menus	$337	$40 $5,840	$6,350
7	**Author**		**$28**	**$23**	**$66**
8	Autho	📋 Copy	$28	$23	$66
9	Group1		**$0** **$0**	**$24**	**$27**
10	Autho	📋 Format Cells...	$0 $0	$9	$9
11	Autho			$15	$17
12	Autho	↻ Refresh	$0		$0
13	**Author**		**$7**	**$293**	**$305**
14	Autho	Sort >	$7	$293	$305
15	**Author**			**$0**	**$0**
16	Autho	Filter >		$0	$0
17	**(blank)**				
18	(blank	✓ Subtotal "Author Name2"			
19	**Grand To**				**$6,748**
20		Expand/Collapse >	⊹ Expand		
21			⊟ Collapse		
22		🗗 Group...			
23		🗗 Ungroup...	⊹ Expand Entire Field		

To collapse just one group at a time click on the minus sign next to the group name.

Expand Groups

To once again see the details for each group, right-click on a group name and then choose Expand Entire Field from the Expand/Collapse secondary dropdown.

To expand just one group, click on the plus sign next to the group name.

Clear Pivot Table

To start over, go to the Actions section of the PivotTable Analyze tab and use the Clear dropdown to select Clear All.

Remove Filters

If you have filters applied to your pivot table and you want to remove all of them, you can go to the Actions section of the PivotTable Analyze tab and choose Clear Filters from the Clear dropdown.

This will remove all filters from the pivot table, including the ones on your Column and Row Labels.

Refresh Pivot Table

If the data that is feeding into your pivot table changes, you need to refresh the pivot table.

To do so, go to the Data section of the PivotTable Analyze tab, and click on Refresh.

You can also use Alt + 5. (I just never remember it.)

The dropdown for Refresh has a Refresh All option which will refresh all data sources in the workbook. You can use this if you have multiple pivot tables that need refreshed.

If you change existing values in your data table or add new rows or columns into the middle of it, Refresh should work to update your pivot table or pivot table field choices.

But if you instead add data outside of the prior data range, then use the Change Data Source option right next to Refresh instead. That will bring up a dialogue box showing your current data selection. You can then change that range to include your new data.

* * *

Okay. So those are some basic common tasks I often need to perform with respect to pivot tables. Now let's talk about how to format your pivot table.

Pivot Tables – Format

In this chapter we're going to cover how to format your pivot table and the entries in that table. I'm going to start with a few formatting options that I use all the time and then we'll go through and be more systematic about your formatting options.

Value Field Settings Dialogue Box For Values Fields Formatting

As I mentioned above, I use the Value Field Settings Dialogue box to tell Excel what type of calculation to perform on my fields because it's also the best place to format the data in a pivot table.

You *can* just select fields in a pivot table and use the Home tab formatting options or right-click on selected fields and use the Number Format option in the dropdown menu. But the problem with those approaches is that they only apply formatting to those specific entries.

If you expand the data in your table at some point, the new entries will not be formatted that way. So if I start with just Author Name in my table and manually format those entries but then add Currency, all of the new entries will not be formatted.

But if you use the Value Field Settings Dialogue box to format the entries for that field, they will.

So how do you do this?

Open the Value Field Settings dialogue box and click on the option for Number Format in the bottom left corner.

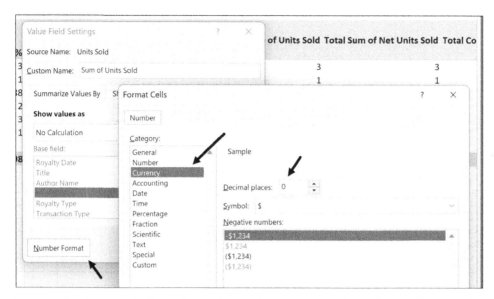

This will open the Format Cells dialogue box where you can then choose how to format the values in that field.

I usually need to do this for currency values to make them look like currency. I will often set the decimal places to zero when I do this to remove clutter from my table.

Subtotals and Grand Totals

Here is a standard complex pivot table that Excel will create by default:

Sum of Royalty	Column Labels											
	2021				2021 Total	(blank)	(blank) Total	2020			2020 Total	Grand Total
Row Labels	January	February	March	April		(blank)		January	February	April		
AUD	25.05	3.79			28.84					2.39	2.39	31.23
Author A	9.96				9.96					2.39	2.39	12.35
Author B	15.09				15.09							15.09
Author D		3.79			3.79							3.79
CAD	27.14	5.75	47.49	23.85	104.23					3.89	3.89	108.12
Author A	27.14	5.75	47.49	23.85	104.23					3.89	3.89	108.12
Author C	0				0							0
EUR	4.22		4.2		8.42			0	7.17		7.17	15.59
Author A	1.66		4.2		5.86				7.17		7.17	13.03
Author C	0				0			0			0	0
Author E	2.56				2.56							2.56
GBP	38.22	33.44	192.11	91.82	355.59			4.85	8.5	4.27	17.62	373.21
Author A	15.44	30.68	188.53	84.74	319.39			4.85	8.5	4.27	17.62	337.01
Author B	22.08	2.76	3.58		28.42							28.42
Author C	0				0							0
Author D	0.35			7.08	7.43							7.43
Author G	0.35				0.35							0.35
INR	0				0							0
Author C	0				0							0
MXN		40.25			40.25							40.25
Author A		40.25			40.25							40.25
USD	334.33	323.88	3079.76	2043.69	5781.66			32.23	89.42	276.26	397.91	6179.57
Author A	296.36	266.15	2934.47	1982.47	5479.45			23.6	74.26	262.4	360.26	5839.71
Author B	3.44	6.88	5.59		15.91				6.88		6.88	22.79
Author C	8.98				8.98							8.98
Author D	22.08	50.85	128.46	61.22	262.61			8.63	8.28	13.86	30.77	293.38
Author E	3.47		11.24		14.71							14.71
Author F	0				0							0
(blank)												
(blank)												
Grand Total	428.96	407.11	3323.56	2159.36	6318.99			37.08	111.37	280.53	428.98	6747.97

If you look across that top row you can see that Excel added subtotals for each year to the table. There's also a grand total row at the bottom.

I often generate pivot tables just to get data to work with, and when I do that I do not want all of that extraneous summary information, I just want the data. So I will often remove the subtotals and grand totals.

To edit your subtotals and grand totals, go to the Layout section of the pivot table Design tab.

The first option there is for Subtotals:

If you just want to remove your subtotals, then click on the Do Not Show Subtotals option.

The other two options you can see there let you decide where to display any subtotals for your rows. By default, at least with my settings, the subtotals show at the bottom of the group. Like here for Group 1:

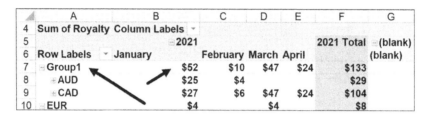

	A	B	C	D	E	F	G
4	Sum of Royalty	Column Labels					
5		2021				2021 Total	(blank)
6	Row Labels	January	February	March	April		(blank)
7	Group1						
8	AUD		$25	$4			$29
9	CAD		$27	$6	$47	$24	$104
10	Group1 Total		$52	$10	$47	$24	$133

You can see the label for Group 1 and then the details for the group and then the Group 1 Total. But in this dropdown you can change that so that the subtotals show on the top instead. Like here where the subtotals for the group now show on the same row as the group name:

	A	B	C	D	E	F	G
4	Sum of Royalty	Column Labels					
5		2021				2021 Total	(blank)
6	Row Labels	January	February	March	April		(blank)
7	Group1	$52	$10	$47	$24	$133	
8	AUD	$25	$4			$29	
9	CAD	$27	$6	$47	$24	$104	
10	EUR	$4		$4		$8	

* * *

Next up is the Grand Totals dropdown:

You can choose to have grand totals for rows only, columns only, both, or neither. If I plan on using the data in my pivot table for a chart (not a pivot chart, but just a basic chart), I will turn them all off. Because what I want is a header row with just data underneath.

Here is that same table from above but now with no subtotals or grand totals.

Sum of Royalty	Column Labels							
	2021				(blank)	2020		
Row Labels	January	February	March	April	(blank)	January	February	April
AUD								
Author A	$10						$2	
Author B	$15							
Author D		$4						
CAD								
Author A	$27	$6	$47	$24			$4	
Author C	$0							
EUR								
Author A	$2		$4				$7	
Author C	$0					$0		
Author E	$3							
GBP								
Author A	$15	$31	$189	$85		$5	$9	$4
Author B	$22	$3	$4					
Author C	$0							
Author D	$0			$7				
Author G	$0							
INR								
Author C	$0							
MXN								
Author A		$40						
USD								
Author A	$296	$266	$2,934	$1,982		$24	$74	$262
Author B	$3	$7	$6				$7	
Author C	$9							
Author D	$22	$51	$128	$61		$9	$8	$14
Author E	$3		$11					
Author F	$0							
(blank)								
(blank)								

Pivot Table Display Options

I can't use the pivot table in that image above as a data table. Right? If I copied and pasted it right now I'd have my values split across multiple rows. The currency for each entry isn't on the same line as the author name or results.

I can fix that though using the Report Layout dropdown menu:

Your three main formatting options there are Compact Form, Outline Form, and Tabular Form. The thumbnail image next to each one tries to show what it would look like, but I often just apply them to see which one I want.

Below that you have the option to either Repeat All Item Labels or not.

If I'm trying to turn a pivot table into a data table, I choose Repeat All Item Labels and Tabular Form. That gives me this:

	A	B	C	D	E	F	G	H	I	J
4	Sum of Royalty		Year	Month						
5			2021	2021	2021	2021	(blank)	2020	2020	2020
6	Currency	Author Name	January	February	March	April	(blank)	January	February	April
7	AUD	Author A	$10						$2	
8	AUD	Author B	$15							
9	AUD	Author D		$4						
10	CAD	Author A	$27	$6	$47	$24			$4	
11	CAD	Author C	$0							
12	EUR	Author A	$2		$4				$7	
13	EUR	Author C	$0					$0		
14	EUR	Author E	$3							
15	GBP	Author A	$15	$31	$189	$85		$5	$9	$4
16	GBP	Author B	$22	$3	$4					
17	GBP	Author C	$0							
18	GBP	Author D	$0			$7				
19	GBP	Author G	$0							
20	INR	Author C	$0							
21	MXN	Author A		$40						
22	USD	Author A	$296	$266	$2,934	$1,982		$24	$74	$262
23	USD	Author B	$3	$7	$6				$7	
24	USD	Author C	$9							
25	USD	Author D	$22	$51	$128	$61		$9	$8	$14
26	USD	Author E	$3		$11					
27	USD	Author F	$0							
28	(blank)	(blank)								
29										

I can now select the whole worksheet, use Ctrl + C to copy and then Paste Special – Values to replace my pivot table with a data table. I will still have to change that top two rows of the table into one row that combines month and year data, but this gives me a summarized data table I can use to create an ordinary chart.

Here that is:

	A	B	C	D	E	F	G	H	I
			January-	February-	March-	April-	January-	February-	April-
2	Currency	Author Name	2021	2021	2021	2021	2020	2020	2020
3	AUD	Author A	9.96					2.39	
4	AUD	Author B	15.09						
5	AUD	Author D		3.79					
6	CAD	Author A	27.14	5.75	47.49	23.85		3.89	
7	CAD	Author C	0						
8	EUR	Author A	1.66		4.2			7.17	
9	EUR	Author C	0				0		
10	EUR	Author E	2.56						
11	GBP	Author A	15.44	30.68	188.53	84.74	4.85	8.5	4.27
12	GBP	Author B	22.08	2.76	3.58				

Note that there is a chapter on pivot charts later in this book if you don't want to do what I just did. Pivot charts let you build a chart directly from a pivot table. Which has the added benefit of remaining dynamic and adjusting as your data changes and you refresh your pivot table. Of course, that can also sometimes be a detriment. I often do that Paste Special – Values trick so that I lock in my values and don't inadvertently delete or change data that is flowing into my charts or calculations.

* * *

Okay. So those are the formatting options I use often with pivot tables in Excel. I format the entries in the Values section, I remove subtotals and grand totals, and I convert the table so that it can be copied and pasted-special and I have a good, working data table.

But there are many more formatting options than that. And it's time to walk through them.

Blank Rows

The final dropdown menu in the Layout section of the Design tab that we haven't covered yet is Blank Rows:

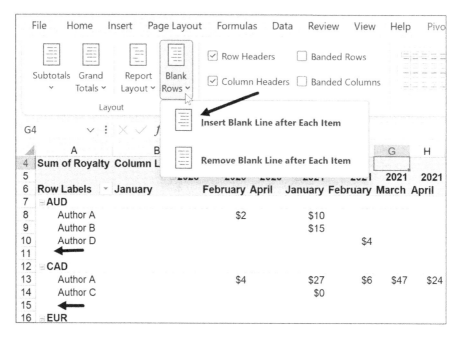

Blank Rows will let you insert a blank row after each "item". In this screenshot above an item is a group, so you can see blank rows that were inserted at Row 11 and Row 15.

I never use this one, but you might want to use it if you need a bit of visual separation between each of your top-level groups in your pivot table. It tends to break the visual of your data as you scan downward so that groups are more distinctive.

PivotTable Style Options and PivotTable Styles

Now let's look at the PivotTable Style Options and PivotTable Styles sections of the Design tab.

I'm going to skip to the styles first. I want to click on that down-pointing arrow with a line above it in the bottom right corner there as seen in the screenshot above. What that does is expands that section to show more styles:

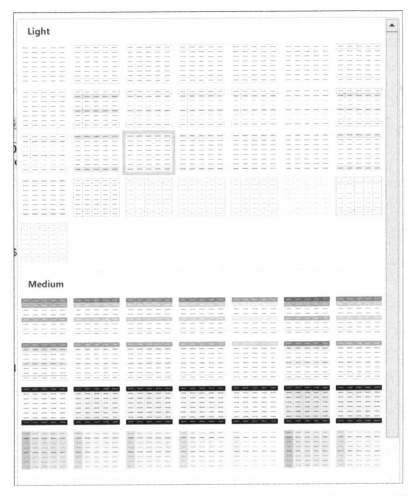

This will probably be a little hard to see in black and white print but essentially what you're seeing here are about sixty different pre-formatted pivot tables. Some have darker colored bands for the header row, some don't. Some use colored bands for subtotal rows, some don't. Some section off the first column, some don't.

There are a lot of choices. And if you scroll down you can see even more.

You can also see that the default style we've been working with so far is one of the choices in the Light section, in the third row. (As of December 2022.)

Hold your mouse over each style in the dropdown and Excel will show you in your worksheet what that style will look like. Click on the style to actually apply it.

Here I've applied Light Blue, Pivot Style Medium 6. (You can see the name when you hold your mouse over each option.)

	A	B	C	D	E	F	G	H	I	J
4	**Sum of Royalty**	Column Labels ▾								
5		▪2020	2020	2020	▪2021	2021	2021	2021	▪(blank)	Grand Total
6	Row Labels ▾	January	February	April	January	February	March	April	(blank)	
7	▪AUD									
8	Author A		$2		$10					$12
9	Author B				$15					$15
10	Author D					$4				$4
11										
12	▪CAD									
13	Author A		$4		$27	$6	$47	$24		$108
14	Author C				$0					$0
15										

It has a little more substance to it than the default style. Also, that extra formatting helps distinguish the values in the table.

Once you've applied a style, you can then use those checkboxes in the PivotTable Style Options section to add or remove row headers, column headers, banded rows, and banded columns formatting. The best way to see what it will do is just check and uncheck those boxes.

Custom Pivot Table Formatting

What if none of those options really give you what you want? Click on the New PivotTable Style option at the very bottom of the dropdown to bring up the New PivotTable Style dialogue box where you can customize everything to your heart's desire:

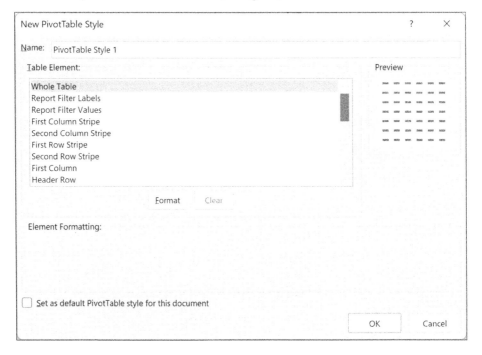

We are not going to go any further down that rabbit hole in this book. Suffice it to say it exists and if you really feel inspired it is there for you to use.

Pivot Tables – More Advanced Analysis

Okay, so I covered some very basic sorting, filtering, and grouping already which is where I spend 98% of my time when dealing with pivot tables, but there's more you can do.

So let's cover that part now. To do this, we need to go to the PivotTable Analyze tab and look at the Filter and Calculations sections.

Slicers

The first choice in the Filter section is Insert Slicer. Click on that and an Insert Slicers dialogue box will appear that lists all of your available fields.

Slicers will sit on top of your workspace and work much like the filter options, letting you pick and choose which values appear in your pivot table. Here I've chosen to show them for Month and Year:

Sum of Royalty	Column Labels								
	2020	2020	2020	2021	2021	2021	2021	(blank)	Grand Total
Row Labels	January	February	April	January	February	March	April	(blank)	
AUD									
Author A		$2		$10					$12
Author B				$15					$15
Author D					$4				$4
CAD									
Author A		$4		$27	$6	$47	$24		$108
Author C				$0					$0
EUR									
Author A		$7		$2		$4			$13
Author C	$0			$0					$0
Author E				$3					$3
GBP									
Author A	$5	$9	$4	$15	$31	$189	$85		$337
Author B				$22	$3	$4			$28
Author C				$0					$0
Author D				$0			$7		$7
Author G				$0					$0
INR									
Author C				$0					$0
MXN									
Author A				$40					$40
USD									
Author A	$24	$74	$262	$296	$266	$2,934	$1,982		$5,840
Author B		$7		$3	$7	$6			$23
Author C				$9					$9
Author D	$9	$8	$14	$22	$51	$128	$61		$293
Author E				$3		$11			$15
Author F				$0					$0

Year
2020
2021
(blank)

Month
January
February
March
April
(blank)

You can left-click and drag each box to move it, which I've done here to place the two slicers to the right-hand side of the pivot table.

Now that they're there I can click on those options to manipulate my pivot table. Here I've chosen to only display information for January 2020:

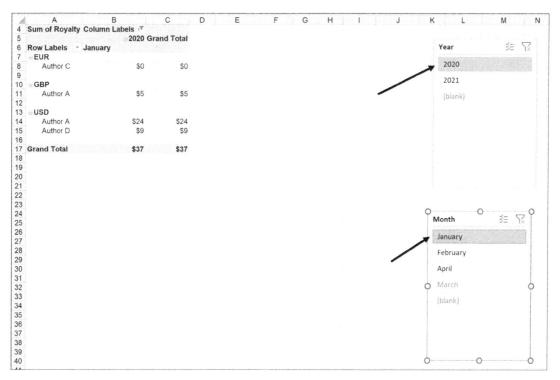

Note that the slicers stay where you've positioned them, but the pivot table, being dynamic, shrinks to only show my limited values. Keep this in mind if you feel tempted to move your slicers around when your pivot table is filtered, because as soon as I remove my filtering, that pivot table is going to go back to taking up that entire space once more.

To select January and 2020, I just clicked on them in each slicer.

But if you want to select more than one value in the slicer, you either need to use Alt + S or click on that icon with the checkmarks and lines next to them at the top of the slicer for that field. (See below. Alt + S basically turns that on.)

What you need to do at that point will depend on whether you've already selected a value or not. If all values are still selected, then as you click on a value it will be *unselected*. If you had already clicked on one value and then realized you wanted more than one, as you click on values they will be selected.

So pay attention to whether a field is shaded (like January and 2020 are in the last screenshot), or not. The shaded ones are the ones you're seeing results for.

To remove any applied filters from a slicer, use Alt + C or click on that little filter with an X on it in the top right corner of each filter. (Alt + C will only work if you select the filter first.)

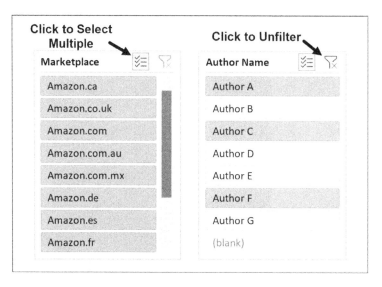

Another option is the Clear Filters option in the Clear dropdown in the Actions section of the PivotTable Analyze tab that we covered previously but remember that will remove all filters in your pivot table as well as all of your slicers.

Slicers remain visible even when you're not clicked onto the pivot table. The advantage to using them over putting a field into the Filters section is that when you have multiple values selected but not all values, you'll be able to see which ones. Also, it's much more intuitive for users to just click on what they can see as opposed to try to use dropdown menus.

Timeline

Next to the slicer is another option, Insert Timeline, which is specific to fields that are dates.

I find this one very tricky to work with, because it doesn't always recognize dates in my data as dates.

For example, I've been showing you anonymized data from an Amazon report. There is a Date field in that data, but when I used that field, Excel told me it was not a date field. Okay, fine. I went back to that data and formatted it as a date. Still not a date field according to Excel. Okay…I copied and pasted special values into a new worksheet and then formatted as a date. Still not a date according to Excel.

Next, I used the DATE function to build a date. Finally, that worked. Excel saw that as a date.

But…weirdly enough, when I added the Date field to my pivot table it would only display the dates in the table as their month. Even when I tried to change the format.

Good news, though. The Timeline option let me filter the data by day of the month, year, and quarter, so even though I couldn't get that information to display in the table itself, I could filter by it.

Here's that table with the timeline set to DAYS to show the days of the month I could filter by:

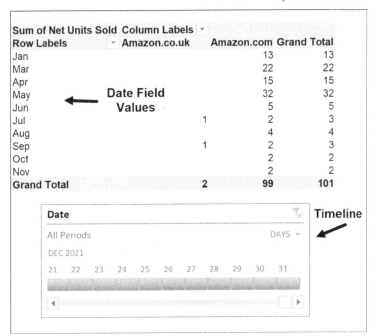

I can change the available choices in the timeline by using that dropdown there that currently says DAYS and setting it to YEARS, QUARTERS, or MONTHS.

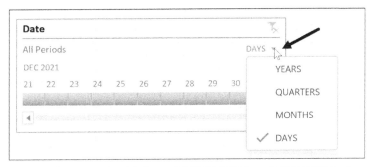

As that changes from DAYS to YEARS to QUARTERS to MONTHS, the available options also change to reflect that choice.

From what I can tell, the available choices will cover the date range from first date to last date, so especially with DAYS, even if there are no results on a particular day it will still show that date as an available option in the timeline if it's between the first and last dates in your data. For example, as you can see above in the pivot table there are not dates in December in this data, and yet the timeline shows December dates to choose from.

Click on any of those values to filter your table. Here I've changed it to YEARS and chosen 2021:

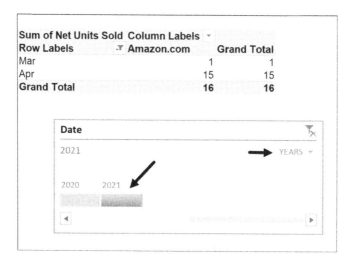

From what I can tell, it's not possible to choose date values that aren't connected, but you can click on one entry, hold down the Shift key and click on a later entry to select a date range, like I've done here for January 1 through 8, 2020:

Sum of Net Units Sold	Column Labels	
Row Labels	Amazon.com	Grand Total
Jan	13	13
Grand Total	**13**	**13**

Note also that there is a scroll bar below the entries in the timeline so that if there are more available entries than you can see, you can scroll right or left to see the rest of them.

To remove a filter from your timeline, click on the funnel with the X in the top corner. Or use the Clear Filters option in the PivotTable Analyze tab.

Okay, that's the timeline. Don't feel bad if it doesn't work well for you, because it never does for me.

Format Your Slicer or Timeline

First, because we haven't covered this yet, to remove a slicer or a timeline, just click on it and then use the Delete key.

If you want to format your slicer or timeline, you can do so. When you insert a slicer or timeline there will be a menu tab up top that says Slicer or Timeline that has pre-formatted style choices as well as a new style option at the bottom of that list. Here is the one for the Slicer:

More interesting to me is the right-hand side of that tab for any slicer, because it includes a Buttons and Size section.

Size lets you specify the size of your slicer. Buttons lets you change the size of the options in the slicer or timeline and also display them in multiple columns, which can be very useful when there are a lot of potential values, like here where I've changed it to show the values in two columns instead of one:

The timeline option does not allow that, it's very basic in terms of how it shows values. But you can at least change the size and the colors used if you want.

Calculated Fields

I will often want to take the values from a pivot table and do further analysis with them. Usually what I do is copy and paste that pivot table as special values, which gives me the data but keeps me from having to worry about the pivot table's dynamic nature which can move data around and is also very hard to reference from outside of the pivot table.

But my solution is not ideal, because sometimes you want to be able to look at your data over time and not have to rebuild your calculations every time. In that case, it's a good idea to build the calculations directly into the pivot table.

The way to do this is by using Calculated Fields. Let's walk through how to do that now.

Go to the Fields, Items, & Sets dropdown menu in the Calculations section of the PivotTable Analyze tab and choose Calculated Field.

This will open the Insert Calculated Field dialogue box:

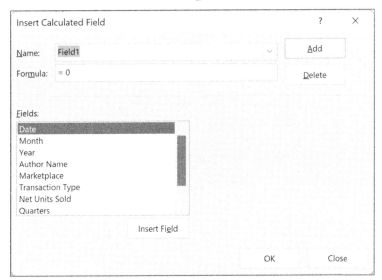

First step, name the field. I usually don't include spaces, so I'm going with RevPerUnit.

Next step is to build the formula. We're going to stick with simple math here. What I want is the Royalty field divided by the Net Units Sold field.

So I click into the formula field, delete the 0, go to the Fields section, find Royalty, double-click on it to insert (or click on it once and then click on Insert Field), type a / for division into the formula field and then go and do the same for Net Units Sold.

That gives me this:

When I'm done, I click OK.

Excel automatically inserted the field into the Values section for me. But it's also now part of the list of fields I can choose from to insert into my pivot table, so I could use it as a filter, for example, just as easily.

Now, because I used division, some of my results came back as #DIV/0! results so it's not pretty right now:

	A	B	C	D	E
4	**Sum of RevPerUnit**	**Column Labels** ⌄↑			
5		⊟**2020**	**2020**	**2020**	⊟**2021**
6	**Row Labels** ⌄	**January**	**February**	**April**	**January**
7	⊟**AUD**				
8	Author A	#DIV/0!	$2	#DIV/0!	$5
9	Author B	#DIV/0!	#DIV/0!	#DIV/0!	$5
10	Author D	#DIV/0!	#DIV/0!	#DIV/0!	#DIV/0!
11					
12	⊟**CAD**				

But I can maybe modify that calculation. How to do so is not intuitive. What you do is go back to that dropdown and choose Calculated Field again and then for the Field Name you type in the exact same name as before. That will change your option for that field from Add to Modify. Type in the new formula you want, click on Modify, and then OK.

The formula I was able to get to work for this was:

=IF(ISERROR(Royalty /'Net Units Sold'),0,Royalty /'Net Units Sold')

It wasn't exactly what I wanted because I'd rather display a blank space than a zero value, but at least it got rid of those error messages.

	A	B	C	D	E
4	Sum of RevPerUnit	Column Labels ▾↑			
5		⊟ 2020	2020	2020	⊟ 2021
6	Row Labels ▾	January	February	April	January
7	⊟ AUD				
8	Author A	$0	$2	$0	$5
9	Author B	$0	$0	$0	$5
10	Author D	$0	$0	$0	$0
11					

(I know we haven't covered a lot of functions yet, but if you're curious about what I used there it was a combination of the IF function and the ISERROR function. Both are covered in the next book in this series or you can look them up in Excel's help.)

And, one more tip on this, if you ever need to see the formula you used for a calculated field, choose the List Formulas option. That's going to show you a new worksheet with all of your formulas in the order that they calculate.

It also has the added benefit of showing each formula so you can copy it if you need to make a small edit and don't want to try to recreate it from scratch. (I was unable to edit the formula directly on that worksheet, which would've been nice, but does not seem to be possible, at least not with fields that have spaces in their name.)

In general, I would recommend keeping your calculations simple in your pivot table, but again, you do you. If you can make it work, good on ya.

Conditional Formatting

While we're here talking about more advanced analysis, let's dip a toe in on applying conditional formatting to our pivot table entries. This is not something I have done a lot of in the past so I can't tell you how it will go wrong. But I can tell you how to do it.

Create your pivot table, select the cells that are in the main body of the pivot table, and then apply your conditional formatting like you would to any other cells.

I recommend that after you do that you go to Manage Rules and choose to edit the rule you just created. When you do so there will be an additional choice you can make:

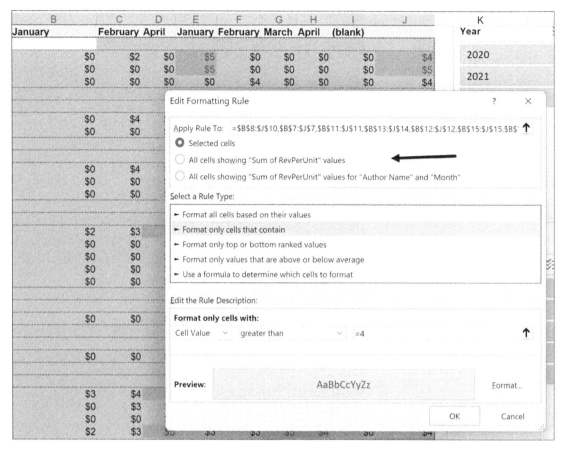

Right now if you look at the Apply Rule field you can see that Excel is using my selected data range. But I can check the box below that, which currently says "All Cells Showing Sum of RevPerUnit Values", to have it apply the rule to my field instead of those specific cells.

That way if the table updates I won't lose the conditional formatting for that field.

If I want to make sure the conditional formatting isn't lost, but also want to limit it to this specific combination that exists, I can check that last box which currently says, "All Cells Showing Sum of RevPerUnit Values for Author Name and Month". That way, if I use the RevPerUnit field in some other part of the pivot table it won't bring that conditional formatting with it.

Here I was able to add separate conditional formatting to two fields (Sum of Net Units Sold and Sum of Royalty) that I had in a pivot table:

	A	B	C
1			
2			
3			
4		Column Labels	
5		2021	2021
6		January	January
7	Row Labels	Sum of Net Units Sold	Sum of Royalty
8	USD	194	334.33
9			
10	GBP	16	38.22
11			
12	CAD	8	27.14
13			
14	AUD	5	25.05
15			
16	EUR	3	4.22

The trick was, or at least the way I got it to work, was to click into one cell in each column, add conditional formatting, and then edit the rule to expand it to all of that field not just that one cell.

It did take a little fiddling, so if it doesn't work the first time, don't give up. Alright, now let's talk for a moment about Pivot Charts.

Pivot Tables – Pivot Charts

Pivot charts did not always exist, so my default still tends to be old-school charts that I've been using for decades. But I've been experimenting enough with these that I feel comfortable mentioning this possibility to you.

What are pivot charts? They are the ability to create a chart straight from the data in a pivot table.

Here I have a very basic pivot table:

	A	B	C	D	E	F
1						
2	Currency	USD				
3						
4	**Sum of Royalty**	**Column Labels**				
5		2021	2021	2021	2021	Grand Total
6	**Row Labels**	January	February	March	April	
7	Author A	296.36	266.15	2934.47	1982.47	5479.45
8	Author D	22.08	50.85	128.46	61.22	262.61
9	Author B	3.44	6.88	5.59		15.91
10	Author E	3.47		11.24		14.71
11	Author C	8.98				8.98
12	Author F	0				0
13	**Grand Total**	**334.33**	**323.88**	**3079.76**	**2043.69**	**5781.66**
14						

It shows four months of data for six authors for one currency. This type of data lends itself well to a column or bar chart, so let's try to create one of those using the PivotChart option located in the Tools section of the PivotTable Analyze tab.

Click on PivotChart and it will bring up the familiar Insert Chart dialogue box:

What I usually find at this point is that my pivot table is not set up the way that I want it to be for that particular chart. I don't know if you can see that here, but the Clustered Column chart it's showing has the four months for each author clustered together. But what I really want is all of the authors clustered together for each month.

I have two options here:

First, I could go back and fix my pivot table by swapping Author Name and Year and Month so that Year and Month are in the Rows section and Author Name is in the Columns section. If I want to do that, I click Cancel.

Second, I can go ahead and create the chart as-is and then fix it from there. I usually choose to fix it from there. So I click OK to go ahead and create my chart.

Once the chart is created, I can go to the Design tab and choose Switch Row/Column, which will fix the chart. *It will also change your pivot table* as you can see here:

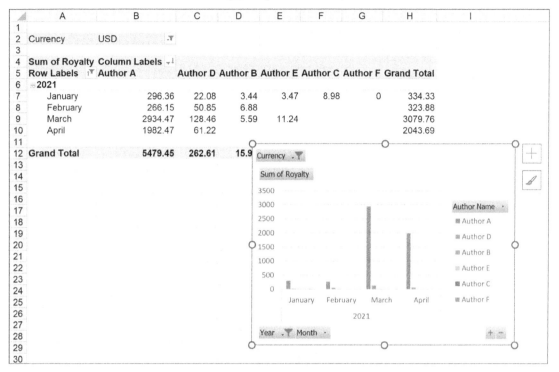

Looking at that chart, one author sort of drowns out everyone else so maybe a stacked column chart would be a better choice. At this point making that change is just like working with any other chart. I go to the Design tab, choose Change Chart Type, and then select my new chart type. Better.

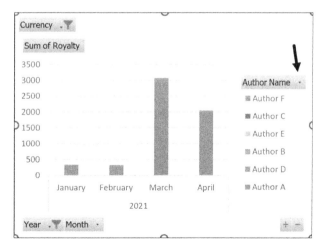

Or maybe I just don't need that author in the chart. If I click on the arrow next to Author Name (see the screenshot above) that will bring up a dropdown menu that lets me choose which values to include in the chart.

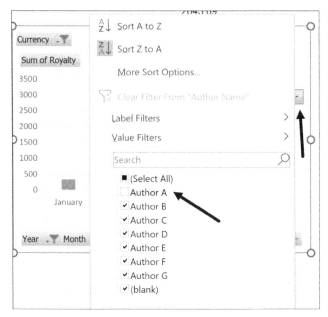

Above you can see that I unchecked Author A. Each field that's being used in the pivot table is available to select or not select. You can also use search, value filters, and label filters.

Here is the updated chart which shows far more detail for all of the other authors now:

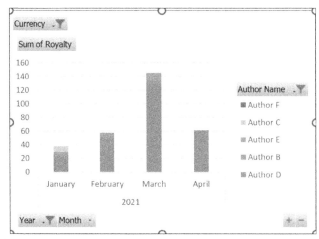

If you look at that chart you'll see that there are other fields you can filter directly on the chart such as Currency, Year, and Month.

Any changes you make to those filters will also be reflected in your pivot table. And vice versa. You can't change one without changing the other. You can, however, create a pivot chart, copy it, and then paste it as a picture to keep that chart you created without having it be impacted by future changes to the pivot table.

The same Chart Styles and formatting options exist for pivot charts as do for regular charts through the Design and Format tabs available up top when you click on your chart.

I find pivot charts to be more interactive than standard charts because of the ability to filter. So if I want to look at say, trend in sales over time for different authors or different series where I have too much data for one chart, rather than create six separate data tables and the charts to go with them, I can create one pivot chart and then quickly cycle through a subset of my data by using that filtering ability.

Just remember that your pivot chart is tied to your pivot table until you lock it in place as a picture. If the chart is being used for some sort of board reporting or regulatory reporting or something where it matters that it be fixed in time, do not leave it as a pivot chart. Lock it down. And, honestly, I'd lock down the data, too, but that's just me.

Okay. A few clean-up items and then we'll finally be done with pivot tables.

Pivot Tables – A Few More Items

Just a little bit of housekeeping before we wrap up this very extensive topic.

Move Pivot Table Values

You can move pivot table values around. So, for example, in my pivot table with Authors A, B, C, D, E, and F maybe I want authors A and E next to each other because they're the same genre.

To move a pivot table value, right-click on it and use the Move secondary dropdown menu to move the field to the beginning, up one, down one, or to the end. You can also use this option to move the field from columns to rows or from rows to columns.

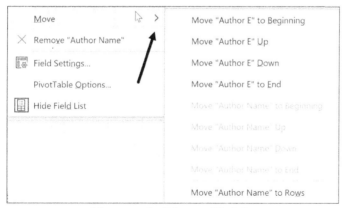

Name A Pivot Table

In the PivotTable Analyze tab there is a section on the left-hand side called PivotTable. You can name your pivot table there if you want to. I never have, but I do believe there are some advanced-level tasks in Excel that are easier if you name your pivot tables.

PivotTable Options

That same section also has an Options dropdown where you can click on Options to open a PivotTable Options dialogue box which contains a number of settings for that specific pivot table:

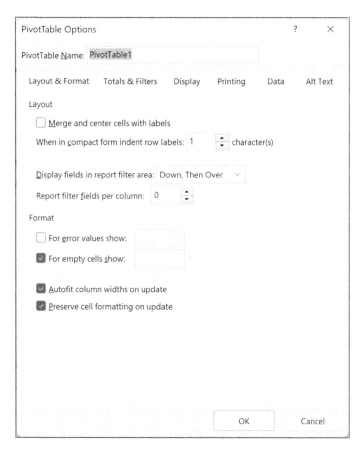

On the Totals & Filters tab you can turn off showing grand totals. On the Display tab you can choose the default sort order for data in your pivot table. On the Printing tab you can set print titles to select what prints at the top of each page or left-hand side of each page. On the Data tab you can set the pivot table to refresh each time you open the Excel file. And more. If you're curious, it's worth clicking through.

PivotTable Options is also available by right-clicking on the pivot table and choosing PivotTable Options from the dropdown menu.

Move PivotTable

In the Actions section of the PivotTable Analyze tab there is an option to move your pivot table. Click on that and you can either move the pivot table to a different location in an existing worksheet or to a new worksheet. Choose the new location based upon where the top left corner of the table will be. It doesn't take into account any filter fields you may have above that.

Recommended PivotTables

If you're not sure what pivot table you want to build or how to build one, there is a Recommended PivotTables option in the Tools section of the PivotTable Analyze tab. Click on that and it will take the data you selected for your pivot table and suggest various pivot tables:

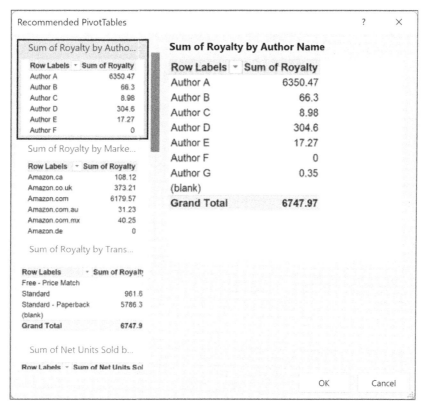

For basic pivot tables the suggestions are solid, but in my case they were all one by one tables. Also, the suggestions covered basically any numeric field combined with any text field which meant that towards the bottom it suggested combinations that made no sense.

But it does at least show you how a basic pivot table is built.

Show Options

At the very end of the PivotTable Analyze tab there are three options in the Show section. Field List turns on and off the PivotTable Fields task pane. Buttons hides or shows the expand/collapse buttons for grouped data or when you have multiple data levels. Field Headers hides or shows the Column Labels and Rows Labels text in the pivot table.

Linking Pivot Tables

It is beyond the scope of this book but Excel has in recent years been upgraded to allow for the linking of various data tables, which can create a data structure akin to what you do in Access or other database tools. That includes pivot tables.

If you want to explore that more, search for help on "work with relationships in PivotTables". It's not an area I've explored enough to give help.

Blank Entries

You may have noticed that some of the example pivot tables I showed you had a "blank" field value as well as the expected values. For me this usually occurs because I just selected the entire worksheet rather than a defined area that only had data in it. I usually just hide those entries or ignore them, but if they bother you the solution is usually going to be to be more careful in what data you select before choosing to insert a pivot table. Either that or to delete blank columns or rows from within your selected data.

Remove Duplicate Values

Alright, pivot tables were the last big topic I wanted to cover, but there are a few other intermediate topics that are easy to do and incredibly helpful. The first of those is how to remove duplicate values.

Here, for example, I have some sample data and I want to extract the unique author names from this list:

	A	B	C	D	E
1	Royalty Date	Title	Author Name	Marketplace	
2	2021-01-31	Book Title A	Author A	Amazon.com	
3	2021-01-31	Book Title A	Author B	Amazon.com.au	
4	2021-01-31	Book Title A	Author C	Amazon.com	
5	2021-01-31	Book Title A	Author D	Amazon.com	
6	2021-01-31	Book Title A	Author C	Amazon.fr	
7	2021-01-31	Book Title A	Author C	Amazon.ca	
8	2021-01-31	Book Title A	Author A	Amazon.com	
9	2021-01-31	Book Title A	Author C	Amazon.de	
10	2021-01-31	Book Title A	Author A	Amazon.com	
11	2021-01-31	Book Title A	Author A	Amazon.com	
12	2021-01-31	Book Title A	Author A	Amazon.com	
13	2021-01-31	Book Title A	Author D	Amazon.com	
14	2021-01-31	Book Title B	Author D	Amazon.com	
15	2021-01-31	Book Title B	Author F	Amazon.com	

They've made this option a little hard to find, but it's still there. Click on the column(s) with the data in it where you want the unique values (or combination of values) and then go to the Data Tools section of the Data tab. Right now Remove Duplicates is an icon with a blue bar, white bar, and blue bar stacked with a red X in the corner. It's located in the same section as Text to Columns.

(You can hold your mouse over the image to make sure you have the right one like I did above.)

Click on that image.

If you have more than one column of data in your worksheet, like I do, and you only selected one column, like I did, then you will see a Remove Duplicates Warning that suggests that you expand your selection.

Click on the "continue with the current selection" option instead, and then click Remove Duplicates.

Understand, however, that if you remove duplicates from one column within a range of data like I'm about to do, that it breaks the relationship between that column of data and the other columns of data in that table. It means that data table can no longer be used with that column of information unless you reverse removing duplicates by using Undo.

(I'll show you this in a moment.)

Next, you'll see the Remove Duplicates dialogue box where you can indicate whether your data has headers or not. (Excel will go right to this dialogue box if the column you selected was standalone.)

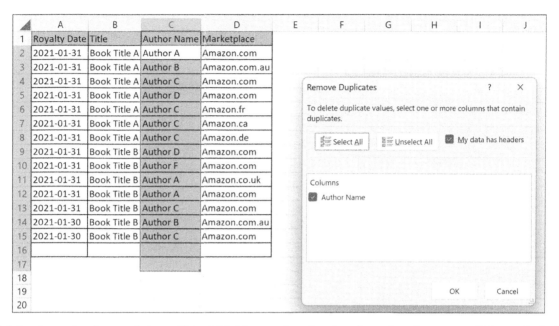

Make that selection and then click OK. If your data has headers, that first row will be excluded from the removing of duplicates. Meaning if my header were Author A and one of my entries were Author A, Excel would keep both.

Excel will then remove the duplicates from your selected column and display a dialogue box that tells you how many duplicates were removed and how many unique values remain. And you'll see that the column of data you used has now been reduced to just the unique values that were in that column.

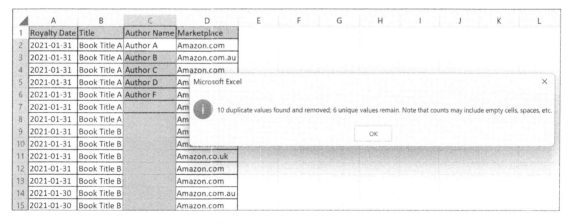

If you selected the whole column like I did, one of your unique values will be the blank cell that you can see in Cell C7 here. So really there are five unique values in my data.

Note here that Row 6 used to be Author C, but because that was a repeat value, you now see Author F listed in that cell. That's what I mean by breaking the relationship between this column and the others. You can no longer trust that the value in that row for that column is the original value that was in that cell.

You can also use more than one column when removing duplicate values. This will give you the unique combinations across columns for your data.

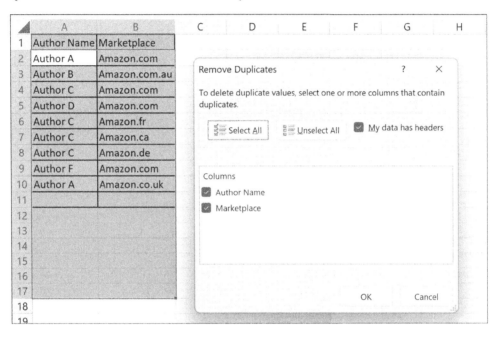

Here, for example, I've removed the duplicate values using both Author Name and Marketplace. (I reopened the Remove Duplicates dialogue box so you can see what that looks like when there's more than one field selected.)

Author C is now listed four times, but only once for each marketplace. When you Remove Duplicates using multiple columns what Excel looks for is unique combinations of the values in those columns.

Once more, be careful here if you have a larger data table. You really can't remove duplicates from some but not all columns in a table without destroying the relationships between the columns in the original table.

Because, once again, even though you're using multiple columns, it still has the same flaw, which is that it will pull up and list all unique combinations with no respect to how they relate to your other columns in your table.

Even if you select the whole table and then uncheck the fields you don't want to consider, it doesn't work. Here is an example where I did that:

It takes until Row 9 to happen, but you can see that the data from the original table on the left is broken in Row 9 when it associates the data in that row with Author F instead of Author D. Because there was already a combination for Author D and amazon.com in Row 5, those values were deleted in Row 9.

If that sounds confusing, bottom-line: Take the column or columns where you want to remove duplicates. Isolate them separate from any other data. And then remove duplicates. If you always do that you'll be fine.

(I'm just too lazy most of the time to do so, which is why I walked through this in the way I did. I like to show others the mistakes I make so they won't make them, too.)

I love remove duplicate values, but this is one of those tasks that can permanently break your data. You can't rebuild a table where one column has had duplicate values removed and the rest haven't. You have to back out of that using Undo to get to the original table.

Which is why it is always a data best practice to keep your original source data somewhere untouched and work on a copy of it so that you always know there's a good version of your data somewhere no matter what you do wrong.

Okay. On to converting text to columns.

Convert Text to Columns

This is another one I've found really useful over the years. On a project a while back I was given a list of employees in the project that was written with the first name followed by the last name. So I had entries for "John Smith" in one cell.

Problem was, John went by Duke, so with the data organized that way no one could ever find him. They were looking under D and he was under J. But everyone knew his last name and could've found him that way just fine.

What I wanted was that same list of names, but sorted by last name. That's where the Text to Columns option comes in. It's very easy to take an entry like "John Smith" and turn it into two columns, one with "John" and one with "Smith" in it.

(I will note here that search, Ctrl + F, could've also been a solution to this issue but that required twenty-plus users with varying degrees of skill to be able to use an Excel file. By splitting the entries into first and last name and then sorting by last name, I could create a printed list of team members for those who didn't want to work with Excel.)

To use Text to Columns, select your cells, and then go to the Data Tools section of the Data tab, and click on Text to Columns.

This will open the Convert Text to Columns Wizard dialogue box:

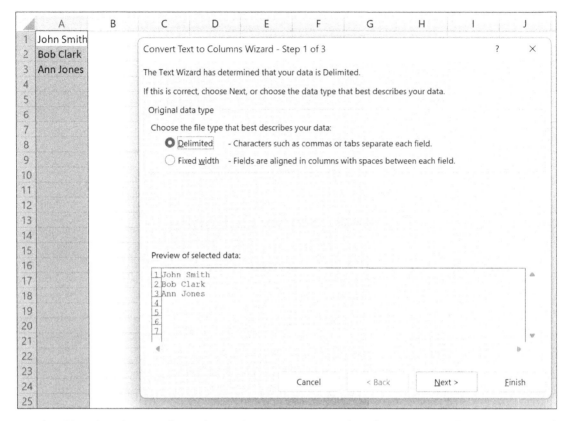

For what I'm showing you here the option you want on that first screen will almost always be delimited.

What delimited means is that the entries you want to separate all differ from one another in terms of potential length ("Joe Smith" and "Vernon McClarick" could be in the same employee list) but that there is a consistent separator between the values (in this case a space).

Fixed, the other option, is for when you're breaking down entries that are all consistently the same size for each section. For example, a social security number is always written as XXX-XX-XXXX so you know exactly where to draw the line each time to split out the first, middle, and last portion of that entry.

For delimited, which is what I'm covering here, click Next and you can then specify how to break the text out.

It will have Tab selected by default. Uncheck that unless your text uses tabs, which is the case with data in .csv files, for example. And then find the character or characters that are separating your text.

In this case, I want to check Space.

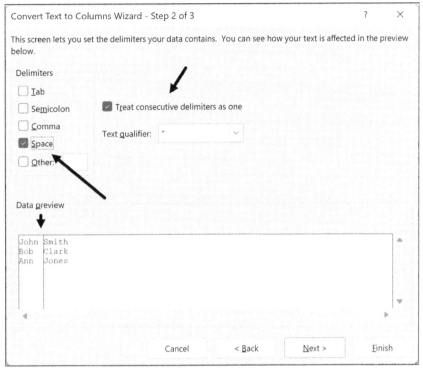

Excel will show you how the data will break in the data preview section at the bottom.

If you have something like "Smith, John" that uses two characters to separate your entries, just check the box for both of them. In this case I'd do so for the comma and the space. And then make sure that the checkbox for "treat consecutive delimiters as one" is also checked.

You can also enter a custom separator in that Other box. So if I have "John Smith-3" and I want to have "John Smith" separated from that 3, I'd want to use a dash (-) as my delimiter.

Whatever delimiter you choose will be deleted. So with "John Smith" I'm going to get a column with John and one with Smith and that space that was between the two words will be gone.

Click Next or Finish once you have your choices made and things look right in the preview screen.

If you click on Next there's a final screen where you can specify a format for each of your new columns. I never use it, but you could if you want to. Click Finish from there once you're done.

Excel will then take the data that was in that column and will split it out into as many columns as it needs using that delimiter you specified.

If you have data in the columns to the right of your entries that is going to be overwritten, Excel will generate an alert to tell you so. You can choose to proceed and overwrite that data or cancel and move that data first. (This sometimes happens for me when I think the text I'm converting will only take two columns but it turns out it takes three because someone has a middle name, for example.)

I find Text to Columns incredibly useful. But...

Not every situation will go smoothly. If you have entries for "Maria Teresa Valdez", "John Smith", and "Hubert Rockford, Jr." all in the same column you're going to run into issues splitting that data into separate columns. The first names will line up fine, but then the Teresa part of Maria Teresa's name will be in the same column as the last names for John and Hubert. And there will be a comma at the end of Rockford. And Jr. in that name will be in the same column as Valdez.

You need to look at your data before and after to make sure that the result you have is what you need it to be.

Also, you may need to combine this task with various Excel functions (like TRIM or TEXTJOIN) to get the final result you want. (Those are covered in the next book in this series, or you can just look them up using Excel's help.)

Additional Tidbits

In this section I'm going to run through a few additional tips or tricks I've picked up over the years.

Fix Number Stored As Text

There are going to be times when you're working in Excel and it gives you an error message or indicates that something is wrong. I cover the formula-related ones in detail in the third book in this series, but I wanted to cover here a different error message that I receive often working with my vendor reports, and that's when numbers are stored as text.

Most of my vendors provide me with .csv reports not Excel files. These days Excel can open those without you even noticing the difference. (In the past you had to have Excel convert them for you.) But sometimes due to the nature of those reports the numbers are not stored as numbers.

Here is an example from one of my vendor reports:

You can see that the top left corner of the cells in Column C all have a green triangle.

When I click on one of those cells, that error triangle appears. Hold your mouse over it and you'll see a dropdown arrow. Click on that to see the menu of options pictured above.

The first line in the dropdown tells you that the error in this cell is that the number is stored as text. You can fix that by clicking on Convert To Number.

If you don't want to fix it, and don't want to see the marks in the corner of each cell, you can choose Ignore Error.

If you're not sure what to do, you can choose to open help through that dropdown by choosing Help On This Error.

In this case, I don't want that value treated as a number. If Excel treats it as a number it will display in scientific notation which does me no good. But often I do need to convert an entire column of values from text to numbers.

To convert all cells in a column at once, select all of the cells first. You should see the warning triangle next to the top cell in the range. Click on the dropdown arrow and select the convert option. That will convert all of the selected cells, not just the top one.

Quick Access Toolbar

If there are tasks in Excel that you perform all the time and you don't want to be bothered to go and track them down in each separate tab, you can add them to the Quick Access Toolbar, which is located at the top of the workspace and always available to you regardless of the tab you're in.

The most reliable way to edit the Quick Access Toolbar is to go to File and then click on Options in the bottom left corner. In the Excel Options dialogue box that appears, click on Quick Access Toolbar.

The left-hand side will show popular commands that you can add to the Quick Access Toolbar. Select the ones you want and then click on the Add option, which will move them to the right-hand side. If you want to remove a task that's already been added, click on it on the right-hand side and choose Remove.

You'll also need to click on the checkbox at the bottom for "Show Quick Access Toolbar" or you won't see your tasks when you go back to the main workspace.

Click OK when you're done.

By default, the Quick Access Toolbar is located below the Ribbon (menu tab options). You can see here that I have a shortcut now for adding new charts:

In the past, the Quick Access Toolbar was located above the Ribbon next to that save icon. That's still where I like it to be.

Just below the checkbox to show the toolbar in the Excel options dialogue box is a dropdown menu for Toolbar Position that you can change to Above Ribbon if you prefer that as well.

Here's what that looks like:

The quicker, but less reliable way to open the Quick Access Toolbar is to right-click on or near the save icon at the very top of the workspace. (I say it's less reliable because there were only about three spots where I could right-click and get this to work. But one of them does seem to be directly on top of the save icon.)

So right-click and you'll see a dropdown menu:

Click on Show Quick Access Toolbar. That will put a small downward pointing arrow that you can then click on to bring up the Customize Quick Access Toolbar dropdown menu

If the option you want as a shortcut is listed in that dropdown (New, Open, Save, etc.), click on it and its icon will be added to the toolbar. If you want more choices, click on More Commands to open the Excel Options dialogue box to the Quick Access Toolbar page.

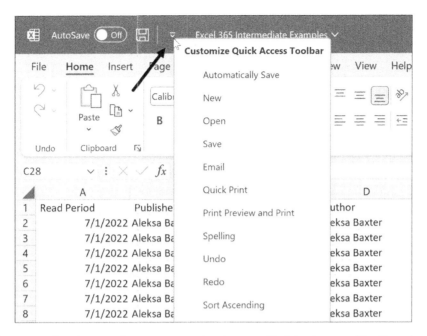

In Excel I personally do not keep any tasks in my Quick Access Toolbar because most everything I use regularly is there on that Home tab, but in Word I do have Page Break and Read Aloud.

I would recommend adding tasks here that you use often but that are kept on a different tab than the one you use most of the time, but not any tasks that you could do with a Control shortcut.

Options

We just looked at one of the things you can do with Excel Options, but there are a large number of ways to customize Excel to your personal preferences.

First, go to File and then click on Options in the bottom left corner to open the Excel Options dialogue box. There are a number of choices there on the left-hand side and then a number of options for each of those choices. (You saw above the page for Quick Access Toolbar.)

This is usually where you can go to fix any weird change that they make to Excel that you're not used to or don't like. And sometimes where you need to go to correct certain things that don't work for you, like me and using (c) for rule citations more than I use it for the copyright symbol.

The one caution I will give here is that the more you customize, the more challenging it becomes to work on a default version of Microsoft Office. (And, for me, the more annoying it is each time I get a new computer and have to set that all up again if I'm using the one-time-purchase versions of Office.)

If you think that you will work at a variety of companies with Office or that you may need to hop onto a colleague's computer to help them out, then I would recommend against extensive customization.

But if you're working for yourself and going to use 365 forever and ever and never need to use anyone else's computer, then make it work for you.

A few examples of what you might want to change on the various pages:

General

- LinkedIn Features section that is checked by default that somehow connects your LinkedIn to your Office account. (Nope.)

- Turn off the Start screen and go direct to a worksheet.

- Change the Office theme (as discussed in *Excel 365 for Beginners*).

- Change default font or font size.

- Change the number of worksheets that are available in a new workbook.

- Turn off the Mini Toolbar and/or Quick Analysis options.

Formulas

- Change Row and Column references to R1C1 format so that columns are also numbered. (Good for when working with macros.)

- Change when calculations are performed.

- Turn off error checking rules.

Proofing

- Add or modify autocorrect options.

- Change dictionary language for spellcheck as well as Spanish and French modes.

Save

- Choose default file format for saving.

- Set how often to AutoSave file.

- Choose default location to save files.

Add-Ins

- Add additional Excel functionality that's not available by default, such as the Analysis ToolPak or Solver.

Zoom

You can zoom in or out on an Excel worksheet. In the bottom right corner there is a slider bar that shows 100% by default. You can click on the vertical bar in the middle of that space and drag to the right to zoom in and to the left to zoom out.

But this only zooms in or out on the cells in the worksheet. Your menu options will not change size nor will any dialogue boxes or dropdowns. To make those more visible you'll need to change your computer settings.

In the Zoom section of the View tab there are also Zoom options.

Click on the 100% icon to return your workspace to a 100% zoom. Click on the Zoom icon to open the Zoom dialogue box which will let you zoom to a specific zoom level.

Zoom to Selection will zoom by default to 400% on the cell(s) you had selected. If the selection is too large for 400% to show all of the entries it will zoom to whatever level will show all of them the best. Be careful using this with a really large selection because it will zoom to the point where the text is not visible.

Conclusion

There's a lot more you can do in Excel. I've dropped a few things from this version of this book that I covered in prior versions like spellcheck and limiting values in cells because I don't think most people need that. But those options do exist.

And there's a whole area of Excel that involves creating connections between worksheets and tables and importing data that I have never included in any of these books. Nor have I ever covered macros. Both are specialized and advanced topics that require a certain level of care or you can create a very big mess.

Also, my target audience for these books are not people who want to wade through that sort of mess. My goal with these books is to give you what you need to be a day-to-day user of Excel not a superuser.

But I do want to let you know that there is a lot more to Excel than I've covered in this book or that I covered in *Excel 365 for Beginners*. And more than I'll have covered by the end of the final book in this series *102 Useful Excel 365 Functions*.

Because if there's something you need, it may very well be there. Excel's help topics are excellent and you should definitely make use of them. (F1 to open the help task pane or go to the Help tab.) They often have videos to go along with the different tasks which are all very well done.

The benefit of these books is that I gave you a path to follow when learning this information. Start here, go there, add this, and here we are. But there's a whole wilderness out there to explore if you want and many knowledgeable sources to draw from.

Don't be afraid to experiment with Excel. Open a new file. Take a copy of some of your data. (Not the original.) And then try to figure it out. Ctrl + Z and Esc will usually bring you back from any mistake you make. But if they don't, close the file without saving, and try again.

Now, having said all of that, formulas and functions are a key part of how I use Excel and we have not covered them in depth yet. That's what the next book in this series is for.

So if you want to continue your learning journey with me, then definitely check out *102 Useful Excel 365 Functions*.

Alright then. That's it. Reach out if you get stuck. I'm happy to point you in the right direction. Good luck with it.

Index

About the Author

M.L. Humphrey is a former stockbroker with a degree in Economics from Stanford and an MBA from Wharton who has spent close to twenty years as a regulator and consultant in the financial services industry.

You can reach M.L. at mlhumphreywriter@gmail.com or at mlhumphrey.com.

Made in the USA
Las Vegas, NV
26 March 2023

69703563R00105